the Volunteer REVOLUTION

Books by Bill Hybels

Becoming a Contagious Christian (with Mark Mittelberg and Lee Strobel)
Courageous Leadership
Descending into Greatness (with Rob Wilkins)
Fit to Be Tied (with Lynne Hybels)
Honest to God?
Network (with Bruce L. Bugbee and Don Cousins)
Rediscovering Church (with Lynne Hybels)

The New Community Series (with Kevin and Sherry Harney)
> *Colossians*
> *James*
> *1 Peter*
> *Philippians*
> *Romans*
> *The Sermon on the Mount 1*
> *The Sermon on the Mount 2*

The InterActions Small Group Series
> *Authenticity*
> *Character*
> *Commitment*
> *Community*
> *Essential Christianity*
> *Evangelism*
> *Freedom*
> *Fruit of the Spirit*
> *Getting a Grip*
> *Jesus*
> *Lessons on Love*
> *Marriage*
> *Overcoming*
> *Parenthood*
> *Prayer*
> *Psalms*
> *The Real You*
> *Serving Lessons*
> *Transformations*
> *Transparency*

BILL HYBELS

the Volunteer REVOLUTION

Unleashing the Power of Everybody

GRAND RAPIDS, MICHIGAN 49530 USA

ZONDERVAN™

The Volunteer Revolution
Copyright © 2004 by Bill Hybels

This title is also available as a Zondervan ebook product.
Visit www.zondervan.com/ebooks for more information.

This title is also available as a Zondervan audio product.
Visit www.zondervan.com/audiopages for more information.

Requests for information should be addressed to:
Zondervan, *Grand Rapids, Michigan 49530*

Library of Congress Cataloging-in-Publication Data

Hybels, Bill.
    The volunteer revolution : unleashing the power of everybody /
Bill Hybels with Lynne Hybels.
      p. cm.
    Includes bibliographical references (p.   ).
    ISBN 0-310-25238-5
    1. Voluntarism—Religious aspects—Christianity. 2. Church work.
I. Hybels, Lynne. II. Title.
    BR115.V64 2004
    253'.7—dc22

2004007230

This edition printed on acid-free paper.

Interior design by Beth Shagene

Printed in the United States of America

05 06 07 08 09 10 /❖ DC/ 10 9 8

---◆---

I often agonize over book dedications. Not this time.
From the day I committed to this project,
I couldn't wait to dedicate it to the volunteer heroes
of Willow Creek Community Church.
They have lived out the
"every-member-a-minister" dream
more robustly than any local church I have ever known,
anywhere in the world.
I know it's supposed to be the leader's job
to inspire and motivate the team.
At Willow, truth be told, the team has motivated and
inspired the leader
more than they will ever know.
I've said it to them hundreds of times,
but I have to express it again right here and right now:
Servants of Jesus Christ at Willow,
I hold you in high regard.
Way to go!

Contents

Acknowledgments

I HAVE NEVER DONE A SINGLE THING OF VALUE WITHOUT THE assistance of others. This book is no exception. The Zondervan team braved a January snowstorm to express their enthusiasm for this project. They are a hearty bunch. Scott Bolinder and Bruce Ryskamp continue to defy the old adage "You can't do business with friends." We've done books together for almost twenty years, and our friendships have deepened. Thanks, guys.

Jim Mellado, President of the Willow Creek Association, applied gentle pressure for years to get me to put some of my reflections on volunteerism into print. God used him more than he knows.

Our Thursday afternoon gang met in my office for months to challenge each others' thinking about volunteers. Their "iron" sharpened mine.

Tammy Kelley, who champions volunteerism at Willow, kept a steady stream of emails flowing my way, reminding me that the church will never reach its full redemptive potential without ever-increasing numbers of fired-up volunteers. Thanks, Tammy.

And finally, my wife, Lynne, immersed herself in the world of Willow volunteers for over a year in an attempt to understand their hearts. Her heart will never be the same. Her writing gifts and editing skills made this book possible, and I am grateful beyond words.

CHAPTER 1

This Is What
I Was Made For

For we are God's workmanship, created in Christ Jesus
to do good works, which God prepared in advance for us to do.

EPHESIANS 2:10

SOME YEARS AGO A NEW STAFF MEMBER OF OUR CHURCH ASKED me how I had the gall to ask people who are already busy at work or in the home to get involved as volunteers at church.

"I mean, don't you feel a little guilty doing this?" he asked. "Isn't it hard to heap such a burden on people?"

He had a point. But I knew of a bigger point:

"During the next few months you're going to meet people who stand at drill presses, ten hours a day, five or six days a week. When they go home at night, few of them sense the pleasure, meaning, and purpose of life they've heard advertised in commercials for beer or computer systems. They're godly, conscientious people, and they feel thankful for their jobs. But they don't find satisfaction for their souls at the drill press.

"And you're going to meet fine, hardworking people in real estate who show thirty homes a week. If they're lucky, one buyer will make an offer, but they're not lucky every week. Many are extroverts who love showing property and helping families find the right home, but even then they probably don't arrive home at night filled with deep inner joy because of their latest showing.

"You'll meet insurance salespeople who have been selling policies for twenty years. While they feel grateful that the insurance business puts food on their table and sends their kids to college, the thought of selling one more policy likely doesn't float their emotional boat.

"You're going to meet car dealers and stockbrokers and bricklayers and police officers and plumbers who, despite their commitment to their careers and jobs, are honest enough to admit that their secular vocation does not offer enough meaning to satisfy the deeper needs that stir in their souls.

"Some of them love their jobs; they feel stimulated and energized by their work. Some of them even leave their workplace each day knowing that they have honored God by their work and their love for people. But few of them would say: *This is what life is all about.*"

I looked directly into the eyes of my young friend. "You and I get to invite these people to be used by God in ways they never imagined. We have the opportunity to empower them to develop gifts they didn't know they had. We can cheer them on as they courageously assume new levels of Kingdom responsibility that fill their hearts to overflowing. And we get to see the look on their faces when they realize God has used them to touch another human being.

"No," I said, "I never really feel guilty inviting people to become volunteers in our church. Never."

ON A MISSION

When the writer of the book of Ecclesiastes decided to determine his purpose in life, he started by accumulating a vast sum of money, only to discover that it didn't provide the meaning he had hoped for. Then he sought power, attained it, and discovered that it too failed to satisfy. Next came a scandalous pursuit of pleasure. Then fame and celebrity. Finally, at the end of all his efforts, he uttered his famous words: "Vanity, vanity, all is vanity." Or as another translation says, "All of this is like chasing the wind."

We were not created to chase the wind.

We are created to join God on a mission. Some people think of God as hanging around beyond the edges of the universe somewhere, listening to really good worship music. The Bible sees it much differently. It teaches that God is at work 24/7, all over our world, filling his followers with grace and mercy and power to reclaim and redeem and fix this broken planet.

It's as if God has work gloves on. And he calls us to roll up our sleeves and join him with our talents, our money, our time, and our passion. He wants his mission to become ours. "If you're into chasing the wind," he tells us, "you can keep right on doing that. Or you can hook up with me, and together we'll transform this hurting planet."

What would it feel like to lay your head on your pillow at night and say, "You know what I did today? I teamed up with God to change the world"?

The desire to be a world-changer is planted in the heart of every human being, and that desire comes directly from the heart of God. We can suffocate that desire in selfishness, silence it with the chatter of competing demands, or bypass it on the fast track to personal achievement. But it's still there. Whenever we wonder if the daily eight-to-five grind or our round-the-clock parenting tasks are all there is to life, that divine desire nudges us. Whenever we feel restless and unsatisfied, the desire whispers in our soul. Whenever we wonder what a life of real purpose would feel like, the desire calls us to something more.

A TRANSFORMED WORLD

Jesus made it pretty clear what God's idea of a transformed world would look like, first within the community of believers called the church and then as the values of that community spread out into the world:

- When he said we should *love the Lord our God with all our heart and soul and mind and strength, and our neighbor as ourselves,* he was calling us to trade a ritualized religion for a genuine love relationship with God and to offer to others the same kind of attention, honor, and compassion we give ourselves.
- When Jesus punctuated his teaching with *concern for the poor, the powerless, and the oppressed,* he was describing a new value system.
- When he said, *Take up your cross and follow me,* he was telling us in graphic terms that following him would require sacrifice, hardship, and death to something selfish inside of us.
- When he said, *Go into all the world and preach the gospel, baptizing in my name and telling people all that you have heard from me,* he was making it clear that his will for us includes the call to worldwide mis-

sion. Our call to love our neighbor as ourselves includes our neighbor across the globe as well as the one next door.

The transformation God longs for transforms everything: marriages, families, friendships, economic and political systems. It lifts up the humble, humbles the proud, and draws people together across racial, social, and cultural divides. It calls us to live in such a way that, as pastor Rob Bell from Mars Hill Bible Church says, *love wins*—in the discussion with our spouse, in the conversation with our neighbor, in the encounter with a stranger, in the decision we make, in the response to one in need, in the attitude toward our enemy . . . in the choice we make to serve.

A POWERFUL MOMENT

When I ask long-term volunteers when they became "lifers"—people who decide to serve in God's mission for as long as he gives them breath—they almost always point back to a specific serving moment that sealed their commitment. "In that moment," they say, "I felt the God of heaven and earth use me, and I discovered that there's nothing in the world like that. It beats anything else I've ever experienced!"

Whether they taught a child how to pray, guided someone toward faith, helped a husband and wife reconcile, served a meal to a homeless person, or produced an audio tape that puts the Christian message in somebody's hand, they knew their lives would never be the same.

Acts 13:36 speaks about the Old Testament character David. It says simply, "And David served the purposes of God in his generation." I love the clarity of that single sentence.

David didn't waste time chasing the wind. He devoted himself single-mindedly to God's mission and died knowing that his one and only life had served its highest purpose.

A PARTICIPANT OR A SPECTATOR?

I've never been a great athlete, but I've played enough to learn that when it comes to sports, it's a lot more exciting to be a participant than a spectator.

For five years in the early '80s, I played with a group of friends in a park district football league. Most of the teams we played against had big guys in construction jobs who hit the bars hard after work. By the time they got to the park, they just wanted to hit people hard.

We church guys weren't big or inebriated, but with speed and deception we did rather well. Several times we won the Tuesday night park district championship.

During those same five years, I served as the chaplain for the Chicago Bears football team. Several times the team gave me premier tickets for games at Soldier Field during the Bears' spectacular charge toward the Super Bowl.

Sometimes on Sunday afternoons or Monday evenings I'd be at Soldier Field, in seats on the fifty-yard-line, watching the world championship Bears cream their opponents. I'd try to focus on the game, but I'd see somebody catch a spiraling pass . . . and I'd wish it was Tuesday night so I could be catching one myself. I'd watch somebody throw a beautiful block . . . and I'd recall the cruncher a big guy put on me the previous week. Despite the bruises I had to show for my participation, I wished I could trade Soldier Field for the hard-packed field at the park district. I wanted to be *in* the action, not just watching it.

My current recreational passion is sailing. Three times, by God's grace, I've had the opportunity to watch the premier sailboat-racing event in the world, the America's Cup. Seated on the deck of a friend's boat in the spectacular waters just north of Auckland, New Zealand, I saw the top racing boats and crews under sail on one racecourse.

But the whole time I thought, *I'd rather participate in one of our local Lake Michigan regattas, on my used, banged-up sailboat with my eight buddies, than be a spectator at the America's Cup Finals.*

Spectating never compares with the thrills and chills of being in the middle of the action. I'd much rather get a little beat up participating in a regatta than sip a lemonade from the comfort of a deck chair on a spectator boat. And I don't think I'm the only one who feels that way.

Every local churchgoer has a choice to make. He can park in his usual spot in the church parking lot, make his way to a comfortable seat in a favorite row, watch a good service, chat with friends, and then go home. That choice makes for a nice, safe Sunday morning experience. Or he can throw himself into an adventure by rolling up his sleeves, joining a team of like-minded servants, and helping to build the local church God has called him to be a part of.

I get letters and emails all the time from volunteers who have discovered that serving is far more satisfying than spectating. Here's an example:

> Three years ago you challenged me to get involved as a volunteer. I was hesitant at first, but you wouldn't let up. Now I can't thank you enough. The meaning I derive, the sense of ownership I feel, the friendships I have built, the spiritual growth I've

experienced—it's all directly related to finding my niche in serving. I will be grateful to you for the rest of my life for inviting me into the game.

Scattered throughout this book you'll find dozens of excerpts from actual emails I've received from volunteers at our church and elsewhere who found the purpose of their lives when they finally committed themselves to serving.

Most of them didn't find the perfect volunteer niche overnight. A lot of them served faithfully in less-than-ideal situations before they discovered what they're really good at. Some of them didn't have a clue where to start. But they started anyway. They experimented. Even though they felt scared or thought they had little to offer, they decided to take a first small step.

A few of those you'll read about tried through the years to silence the voice calling them from self-absorption into servanthood. But God didn't quit. And now they have become the most enthusiastic proponents of serving.

One man wrote the following:

> My life used to be about one thing: me. I was a self-serving guy who had neither purpose nor passion. I was leading a miserable life, throwing away time and money on beer and cheap thrills. Then one day I walked into a church and heard the message of Christ: Give your life away to others and you will find your life. I didn't have much to give up so I decided to give it a shot.
>
> That's when my life started to change and Christ became more real to me. I started serving teenagers and found a purpose . . . a reason for my existence.

It was twenty-one years ago that I wandered into that church. Today my life is richer than I ever believed it could be. Serving others made the difference. It was one of the best decisions I ever made.

Here's the experience of a woman named Marty:

Two years ago I started volunteering in our ministry for children experiencing divorce. I had been divorced myself and clearly remembered what it was like for me as a single parent, struggling with all that was happening in my life and having very little energy left for my children. When I heard about this ministry I was convinced God was calling me to get involved.

Every week I see children come in struggling with anger and fear and leave with hope and peace. How I wish my own kids had been served in this way.

So many people hesitate to volunteer because they are afraid of failing. I felt that way too. But when we let God lead us to where he wants us to serve, we find an incredible sense of satisfaction and joy. I wouldn't give that up for the world.

Why don't I feel guilty asking people to volunteer in the local church? Because I know that what Marty says is true. People who let God lead them to where he wants them to serve find "an incredible sense of satisfaction and joy."

What about you? Is it time for you to get up from the grandstands, crawl over a couple of benches, suit up, and get out on the playing field? I guarantee, it's far more exhilarating to be a participant than a spectator. Why watch others change the world when you can join them?

Your move.

CHAPTER 2

I Can't Believe
I Get to Do This!

Eric knows money. As a corporate and international banker for almost thirty years, he loaned millions and millions of dollars and moved huge piles of it around the world. And he loved doing it. "I never got tired of the challenge," he says. But despite the pleasure and success he found in his work, other dimensions of his life remained underdeveloped and unfulfilled.

Before he went into banking, Eric had worked as a teacher in an inner-city school and had never lost his passion to serve under-resourced children and families. Good thing, because suddenly he found a very needy child living right in his own home.

Karen, Eric's wife, had decided to take in a foster child just after the youngest of the couple's four children turned seven. Eric supported her decision but told her she would have to do it on her own because he was busy banking and traveling.

But fostering quickly became a "family ministry." The eleven babies who lodged in their house and their hearts during the next decade awakened in Eric his earlier interests.

When Eric had the opportunity to take an early retirement, he "left the corporate world to do something more heart-oriented, something I had a passion for." In the years since then, Eric has become what he calls "a professional volunteer."

He and his young adult son had already served two weeks each year doing construction and maintenance at our church camp in Northern Michigan. Eric was also on the *Grounds Team*, which cares for all the landscaping on our church property. And he had begun serving with his wife and daughter in a toddlers Sunday school class.

With more time to invest, he joined one of our *Trades & Engineering* teams, a group of approximately twenty volunteers who meet every other Monday evening for Bible study and small-group experience; on the opposite Monday they serve by making mechanical, electrical, and woodworking repairs throughout the church building, saving the church thousands of dollars each year—dollars that can then be devoted to ministries that directly touch people's lives. "It's a matter of good stewardship," says Eric. "Why should the church spend money on jobs that could be done by volunteers who would love to do it?"

Eric moved even closer to his original passion when he joined volunteer teams providing construction and rehab services to local and international churches and parachurch ministries in low-income areas. He began leading teams on *Extension Ministry Plunges*, weekend opportunities for volunteers from our church to work in partnership with inner-city ministries serving the homeless, at-risk youth, single mothers, incarcerated people, prostitutes, and other needy groups.

"The Bible tells us that faith without works is dead," says Eric. "This is one way we can put our faith into action."

As a member of the advisory board for our *International Ministries*, Eric's expertise in international finances and language, as well as his skills in construction, find a perfect outlet. One week he's crunching numbers at a board meeting at our church. The next week he's pounding nails in a church building in an under-resourced area of Latin America or consulting with one of our Spanish-speaking ministry partners.

Karen also volunteers full time. In addition to caring for foster babies, she serves food every other week to the group of homeless people who stay at our church on Thursday nights. She started doing this because her teenage daughter wanted to, but now she's hooked. "I didn't realize what a thrill it would be to help our guests relax and offer them a little bit of comfort."

Last summer she and her daughter spent a week working at an orphanage in the dusty Baja peninsula of Mexico. "Watching my daughter pass out food, wash and cut hair, and play games and sing songs with kids in a workers' camp of tin shacks was one of the greatest parenting moments of my life."

Karen also volunteers one morning a week at an under-resourced preschool in a community near where she lives. "The teacher is overworked, and she doesn't really enjoy doing 'crafty things.' So I take in all the supplies and teach the kids crafts." On a table in Karen's living room, beside beautiful photos of her grown children and her foster kids, stand snapshots of the preschoolers, proudly displaying their "artwork." Karen can't stop smiling while she flips through the photos.

"I've thought about renewing my physical therapy license," says Karen. The youngest of her four children is nearly grown, and she's currently in between foster babies. "But then I think, Why would I do that? I'm so lucky to be a volunteer. I'm having so much fun!"

"For years," says Eric, "my job was my passion. I worked hard and believed that success had to come out of the corporate world. But that changed. Big time."

In a Christmas letter, Eric's daughter wrote, "Dad, when you retired from banking, you faced a new chapter of your life. This has transformed you into a different person. You have a big heart, which shines every time you return from a project in the inner city or overseas. I can see now what you really have a passion for." That, for Eric, is a new—and improved—definition of success.

THE REWARDS OF VOLUNTEERING

One of my greatest thrills as a leader is to watch people like Eric and Karen discover that God can use their small and mostly hidden acts of love and kindness to change lives, churches, local communities, and eventually the world. I love seeing people live out in their daily lives what I believe wholeheartedly: that volunteers can transform society and at the same time find deep personal satisfaction.

But it can take a long time to change long-held beliefs about volunteerism. Many people believe that volunteerism is more about duty and drudgery than fun and fulfillment.

Sadly, sometimes it is.

Too many willing-hearted volunteers have been wounded "on the job." They've responded to an invitation to serve, only to end up in a volunteer position that was poorly conceived, resulting in tasks that few people would find fulfilling. Or they show up to serve and discover they have nothing to do; an unprepared volunteer coordinator has wasted their time, causing them to lose precious hours they had willingly carved out from their busy schedule.

Some work hard on menial tasks without ever hearing how their efforts serve a grander cause; they're given plenty of work, but no vision. Others have felt overwhelmed by unreasonable demands for which they've not received proper training; rather than being set up to win, they get put on the express lane to frustration and failure.

Many have been hurt when a coercive leader drafted them to "fill a slot" without considering their gifts or talents or what they love to do. Some have given hours—maybe even years—in voluntary service to an organization or church, without receiving a single thanks.

But it doesn't have to be that way. The true-life stories in this book give testimony both to the deep satisfaction volunteers can experience and the profound impact they can have on others. Karen and Eric are not exceptions. I believe the fulfillment they have enjoyed as volunteers should be, and can be, the norm.

My experience with volunteers has come primarily through the church I have pastored for almost three decades. In the early days of our church planting adventure, my staff and I learned some painful lessons about how to, and how not to, treat volunteers. The pain we witnessed in the lives of wounded volunteers compelled us to acknowledge our

mistakes and learn better how to support and encourage
these willing servants.

Over the years we did learn—and we're still learning.
Every month, in fact, senior leaders from our church meet
to ask volunteer questions:

> Are we caring for our volunteers properly?
> Are we providing the right training?
> Is there a better way we could recruit?
> What are the faithful volunteers in our church actually
> experiencing?
> Are they growing spiritually?
> Do they feel like an integral part of a team?
> Are they energized by the overall vision of our church?

Then we talk with volunteers about these issues so we
can learn from their experiences and continue to improve
the volunteer culture in our church. This book grew, in large
part, out of those conversations.

LEARNING FROM THE SUCCESSES

Not everyone has the freedom Karen and Eric have to be
full-time volunteers. But plenty of people have discovered
the rewards of volunteering in the hours tucked between
full-time jobs and full-time parenting. Let me tell you about
a few of the people I know.

Around 7:00 a.m. on a Saturday in November, I drove
into the church parking lot. I saw several teams from our
volunteer grounds crew doing end-of-the-season cleanup of
our church campus, clearing out flower beds, raking leaves,
and planting spring bulbs. Because working on the grounds
crew provides a particularly family-friendly opportunity, I

saw plenty of kids mixed in with the Saturday workers (and volunteer kids often become volunteer adults).

"Every time I drive onto the church property," says one volunteer, "I see the flowers and trees and pond that are so beautiful and peaceful, and I know that the little contribution I make helps to calm people down as they drive on the campus and prepares them to hear God speak to them. I love being part of this."

When I parked, I noticed two dark green semi tractors with forty-foot, shining aluminum trailers parked in the back row of the church parking lot. The rigs belong to one of our church volunteers who owns a food brokerage company; we would use them later in the weekend to transport thousands of bags of groceries to our church food pantry several miles away. Our church attendees regularly rally together to buy groceries, which they leave in bags behind their cars during designated weekend services. Volunteers in pickup trucks gather the bags during services, then load them into the semis.

Some members of our congregation, such as my twenty-something son and his friends, walk up driveways and knock on doors in local neighborhoods, offering people an empty grocery bag and the opportunity to fill it for hungry families in our community. "If you leave a filled bag on your porch tomorrow night, we'll make sure it gets to the people who need it." These young volunteers picked up forty bags of groceries in one evening, which they brought to church and loaded in the semis.

When the semis arrive at the food pantry, additional volunteers unpack the bags and restock the shelves. Hundreds of volunteers get involved in this effort. Another hundred-plus volunteers serve weekly shifts at the pantry, talking, praying, and sharing food with people who often are as spiritually thirsty as they are physically hungry.

Patsy, a vivacious mother of four, helps head up our food pantry. I remarked to her husband, Mike, that since he'd helped Patsy with the mammoth task of relocating the food pantry, and since he's on our ministry reorganization committee, as well as the church board of directors, we must be wearing them out. His response left no doubt in my mind how he and Patsy felt.

"Are you kidding? There would be a hole in our hearts the size of the Grand Canyon if we couldn't serve like this. We don't even want to imagine our lives without it."

Inside the church building, additional Saturday morning servants are at work.

The volunteer sound-and-lighting folks for our junior high ministry have finished their production setup and begun rehearsing for the program they'll present later in the morning. Worship music shakes the floors and the ceilings of their huge meeting room. Somewhere in the mix of people rushing around, shouting out last-minute instructions, and finally praying before the doors open, there is a paid staff member or two. But the band, the production people, and the small group leaders are volunteers; average age: about eighteen. Whatever they do on Friday night doesn't keep them from showing up on Saturday morning to make a difference in the lives of about a thousand junior high students.

Meanwhile, in the main auditorium, volunteers crawl up and down rows, cleaning the backs of the theater-style seats. They do this every Saturday morning in preparation for weekend services. One of the knee-crawlers, Dale, has attended our church for nearly three decades. He's the head of property management for a large real estate company, but he never misses his Saturday morning commitment. Two things bond the seat-cleaners. They laugh a lot, and they pray for the people who will sit in the seats they clean.

In addition to the seat-cleaners, a weekly seat-repairing team fixes wobbly seats. Whatever mess they make with their repairs gets quickly removed by a team with vacuums, which faithfully chases the seat-repairers up and down aisles. (And people think that clean, safe seats "just happen.")

In the bookstore, Grace, seventy-eight, is busy stocking shelves and helping customers. Her husband, Dave, eighty-three, serves in audiotape production. Together, they also lead a couples small group. They started volunteering at church in the early '80s, when Dave still worked full-time as an engineer; they have served in a dozen ministries since then. When they first started, Dave's work and family kept his weekdays filled, but his Saturdays were free. So for ten years he spent every Saturday afternoon emptying all the trash cans throughout the church building (we had no paid janitorial staff at the time). On Sundays, while he waited for Grace to finish her work in the bookstore, he'd wander through the nursery and toddler classrooms, gathering up dirty diapers. He's also served as an engineering consultant on major church construction projects; not long ago I saw him seated at a conference table, carefully examining specifications for an air conditioning system. Despite Dave's ongoing battle with cancer, Dave and Grace refuse to quit serving. "It's the most fulfilling thing we do," they insist.

In another room, Jim and his wife, Lynn, volunteer in a monthly workshop to help new people at the church get connected in small groups and serving opportunities. Jim, who implements and maintains computer systems for a huge recycling company during the week, leads and trains the table facilitators who serve at the Saturday workshops. Lynn, a church staff member, volunteers by offering one-on-one guidance to people seeking the right place to get involved. In addition, Jim and Lynn serve throughout the year by opening their home to international visitors attending conferences at the church. Jim also played trumpet in the church band for almost fifteen years, and Lynn serves with the prayer ministry. When I ask about their volunteer involvement, Jim gets all choked up. "It never gets old," he said. "Serving—we love it. It's our life."

By 8:15 a.m., the *Promisetowne* rooms have filled with infants, toddlers, and kids through age six. While their moms or dads volunteer in various Saturday morning ministries—serving junior high students, helping at a career workshop, leading an Alzheimer's support group, or praying for requests turned in to the prayer ministry—the kids learn and play in a preschool environment run by other volunteers, often teenagers or folks with grown kids. These child-care volunteers are committed to freeing up young parents to experience the joys of serving. Open four days each week, *Promisetowne* has a core of eighty to ninety volunteers who serve nearly a hundred kids each day, enabling many young parents to volunteer throughout the week in the bookstore or the food service center, as administrative assistants to staff, as support group leaders, and elsewhere, touching every ministry of the church.

When we first started our church, we had no money to hire staff. We had a dream . . . and truly, nothing beyond that.

So we all started out as volunteers. At night I brokered produce on the Water Street Market in Chicago for my dad's wholesale produce company. Lynne taught private flute lessons and worked at a Christian bookstore. Others in the original core worked as school teachers, charter bus drivers, rookie real estate agents. We had a tool-and-die maker, a video producer, and a printer. Many of us were still in college. But we felt convinced that if we volunteered our time and talents as faithfully as we could, we could turn our dream into reality.

In hindsight, our lack of funding was probably a huge gift. It forced us to stumble upon a profound truth: the church was designed to be primarily a volunteer organization. The power of the church truly is *the power of everybody* as men and women, young and old, offer their gifts to work out God's redemptive plan.

Jesus deliberately made a strategic decision when he invited Peter, James, John, and the other disciples to help him spread the news of the Kingdom. He could have built his ministry in other ways. He could have remained a solo act. He could have insisted that all of his followers do a two- or three-year full-time missionary stint during their first decade of discipleship.

But Jesus chose to advance his work primarily on the shoulders of ordinary people who live in the real world of family and business and community. He believed the same skills used to make clay pots and herd livestock and bake bread could be used to advance the Kingdom of God.

The apostle Paul felt so strongly about being a volunteer that in 1 Corinthians 9 he reminded people that he himself was one. He supported himself by making tents on the side so that he could serve as a pastor and leader without becoming a financial drain on the church.

I am a paid staff member. And I am grateful beyond words for the gifted, hard-working, creative paid staff with whom I work. But the Kingdom of God cannot advance through the efforts of paid church staff alone. I believe that the church is the hope of the world. But that hope rests on the willingness of volunteers from all walks of life—doctors, teachers, at-home moms, business executives, college students, nurses, grandmothers, retired engineers, carpenters, dentists, hairdressers, high school kids, grocery-store clerks— to be mobilized, empowered, and used by God.

THE POTENTIAL TO MAKE A DIFFERENCE

Over the years I've heard a lot of great servants of God describe themselves as "just a volunteer." Before I write one more page, I want to make something very clear. The term "just a volunteer" should have no place in our vocabulary.

The church I pastor would not exist without the thousands of hours given each month by fired-up volunteers. There's not enough money in the world to pay for all the good deeds desperately needing to be done in the name of God in my church and yours, in my community and yours, in my country and yours.

Without the work hours of volunteers, countless wounds will not be tended, mouths will not be fed, grieving people will not be comforted, broken marriages will not be mended, lonely people will not be embraced, children will not be nurtured. Countless cups of cold water will never be offered in Jesus' name, and countless spiritual seekers will never be befriended and coached toward Christ.

Whether God has blessed you with forty hours a week of discretionary time, or whether you can barely snatch forty minutes a month from your overloaded schedule, you have the potential to make a difference in your corner of the world.

What do you have to offer? More than you probably think. You have the gifts and talents you were born with. The passions that inspire you. The blessings of education. The skills you've honed as you've worked at home or in the marketplace. The life experiences that have matured you. The pain that has deepened you. The love of neighbor that spills from God's heart into yours.

These are powerful tools for good that God has lavished on all his children. Why? So that we can lavish goodness on others. One of my favorite definitions of the church is a "community of blessing"—a community blessed by God so that it can bless the world.

Once you decide to invest even a small portion of the blessings God has given you into the lives of others, you'll find the seed of something powerful sown in your own soul. And someday, in the midst of giving yourself in the spirit and act of volunteerism, that seed will blossom into the amazing realization that *this* is what you were made for!

CHAPTER 3

Servanthood:
The Great Gamble

*We love, serve, and care for others because that is normal behavior
for people who are filled with God's Spirit. We are Christians.
Christ was the ultimate servant. We can't help but serve because
the Spirit of the Servant has filled our hearts. When we serve,
we are just being who we naturally are.*

STEVE SJOGREN[1]

Most of us want to live lives of purpose. We want to give ourselves to a worthy cause. But years of bombardment by the messages of a self-serving culture have confused us. *Indulge yourself. Fulfill your desires. Satiate your appetites. Pursue pleasure. It's all about you.*

Given such messages, it's easy to understand our fear that investing time and energy into serving God and others will diminish our lives. What will really happen, we wonder, if we leave the comfort of the spectator stands and get dirty on the playing fields of servanthood? Won't we be busier than ever and have to work even harder ... without a compensating increase in our bank accounts? And if so, does that make sense?

If I commit myself to serving, we ask, will I end up enjoying it or dreading it? Will life really be more fulfilling?

Or just more draining? Will it help me grow spiritually or might the extra demands actually weaken my spiritual life? Why should I sign up for this? Will it really be worth it?

These questions haunted me in 1972 when I sensed God nudging me to volunteer with a high school youth group in Park Ridge, Illinois. God provided a short, square-bodied college professor named Gilbert Bilezikian to help me find answers.

Dr. B, an Armenian refugee exiled in Paris during his youth, presented his New Testament classes in an elegant French accent—but there was nothing elegant about his message. His radical call to follow Jesus into a life of sacrifice and service absolutely rocked me.

I was a cocky, twenty-year-old thrill-seeker from an affluent family. I'd had boats, private planes, fast cars, and Harley Davidsons at my disposal since long before I could operate them legally. I'd traveled extensively through South America, Europe, Africa. I'd vacationed at the famed Copa Cabana Beach in Rio de Janeiro. I knew what life was about!

But this compact, middle-aged professor had me by the scruff of the neck, shaking all certainty out of me.

"Students," he said, "true fulfillment will never come through self-gratification." While my classmates slept, I broke out in a cold sweat. His words contradicted everything I thought I believed.

"Self-gratification will never lead to the fullness of life you are looking for. It will lead you to emptiness and self-destruction. And along the way, you will destroy other people." I could barely breathe.

Dr. B explained to those of us sitting in his classroom that most people eventually figure out what it takes to get to the top. If they work on Wall Street, the goal is to earn a lot of money. If they work in Hollywood, the upward journey means producing award-winning films. If they're in Washington, D.C., the key is to get as close as possible to the Oval Office.

"We all want to get to the top," he declared, "but Jesus said the way to the top in his Kingdom is to become a faithful servant to the Father and a humble servant to one another."

SERVANT OF ALL?

The decision to become followers of Jesus radically changed the lives of his first disciples. They left their families, friends, and jobs to become homeless travelers, banking their futures on the often-disturbing words of a revolutionary teacher.

For a while, of course, it felt like a grand adventure. Take Peter, for example. Every day for years he had walked down to the seashore, cast off in his boat, dropped the nets, hoisted up a catch of fish and counted them, took them to the market, traded them for a few coins, bought food, and went home. Hardly scintillating.

Then he met Jesus and became the right-hand man to the most powerful, gifted, charismatic leader of the day. Jesus miraculously fed huge crowds, healed the sick, and raised people from the dead. Who could imagine where it might all lead? Peter had fixed himself to a star and the star was rising.

But then things started getting messy. Jesus' habit of boldly challenging the self-serving values of religious and political leaders created hostility. His relentless call to a different way threatened to get his followers in big trouble.

It had always been hard for the disciples to accept Jesus' radical call to serve God and others. "If anyone wants to be first," he told them, "he must be the very last, and the servant of all."

Isn't that a bit extreme?

Then he started using really uncomfortable language: deny yourself, take up your cross, lay down your life.

In Matthew 19:27, Peter finally asked the question all the disciples probably wanted to ask: "We have left everything to follow you! What then will there be for us?"

I'm confident there stirred in Peter's heart a sincere longing to abandon his life to Jesus' cause. But he was only human. His old life, if not an adventure, had at least been predictable. He knew where he was headed and what he'd get out of it. But with Jesus, he had to put everything on the line with no certain return. *Am I a fool to follow this man?* he wondered.

"I tell you the truth," Jesus replied, "no one who has left home or brothers or sisters or mother or father or children or fields for me and the gospel will fail to receive a hundred times as much in this present age (homes, brothers, sisters, mothers, children and fields—and with them, persecutions) and in the age to come, eternal life" (Mark 10:29–30).

Jesus promised Peter that following him would be worth it. It wouldn't be easy—they might even face persecution— but they would receive incredible rewards, both in this life and the next. He actually promised that his followers would receive back a hundred times whatever they gave up!

The Gospels make it clear that the disciples had a hard time believing their leader's promise. They seemed convinced that self-centeredness, not servanthood, provided the only sure pathway to the rich life they longed for.

One day Jesus asked them a question—"What were you arguing about on the road?"—but they kept silent because on the road "they had argued about who was the greatest."

Jesus called his followers to servanthood, but in the unguarded moments of their private conversations, they argued about which of them was most likely to hit the big time. Who among them, they debated, was the most gifted? Who would be the best known? Who would enjoy the most success in the future? Who would get the most speaking engagements, grant the most interviews, sign the most autographs, wield the most power?

You know, we're a lot like the disciples.

THE WAY TO REAL LIFE

I felt so gripped by Dr. B's teachings on servanthood that I asked him to speak to the little high school youth group I had begun leading.

"You want to really live?" Dr. B asked the students. "Then drape a serving towel over your arm." Dr. B hit this theme not once, not ten times, but in nearly every message he presented in those early years of our youth ministry.

He frequently taught the familiar story from John 13 about the day Jesus and the disciples had dinner and the foot-washer didn't show up. In that time and place, where people often walked in sandals down dusty roads and then reclined at low tables with their feet not far from the faces of other guests, custom required that a servant at the door should wash dirty feet. But not so at this dinner. Something went wrong. The foot-washer didn't show up.

Imagine you're standing behind a pane of glass watching this scene. The first disciple enters the upper room and discovers there's no foot-washer. Suddenly, for him, it's decision time. Does he wash his own feet? Does he take off his garment and become like a rank-and-file servant and wash everyone else's feet? Look into his eyes. He's thinking, *Not me. That's not my job. I'm not a slave. I'm no foot-washer.*

He tries to size up where Jesus will sit and chooses an advantageous position at the table.

The second disciple enters, realizes there's no foot-washer and sees his friend already seated at the table. *Well,* he thinks, *if he's not going to stoop to the level of foot-washer, neither am I.* And he heads toward the second-best seat in the house.

All the disciples do the same thing. They file in. Walk past the water basin. Choose the best remaining seat at the table. Recline. Stick their dirty feet in each other's laps.

Last, Jesus enters. Watch him. He looks at the water. He looks at the filthy feet of the disciples. You can see it in his eyes. Three years, sermon after sermon, illustration after illustration, confrontation after confrontation. Can you see it? It looks a lot like failure.

He walks to the table and reclines. He just sits there, silently. *Maybe someone will at least have the humility to wash the feet of their master.* But no, nobody moves.

Now watch him. He gets up from the table, walks to the water basin and starts to take off his outer garment. Carefully he picks up the towel and slips it through his belt, exactly the way a common servant would. Then he pours the water into the basin.

Now look at the eyes of the disciples. Disbelief. Embarrassment. Then as Jesus begins to wash the feet of the first disciple, you see something deeper in their eyes: agony, regret, maybe tears. *What is the matter with me? How did I miss this? My whole world revolves around me. It's bad enough I wasn't humble enough to wash the brothers' feet. But I wouldn't even wash my Savior's feet! How could I have done this? What's the matter with me?*

Jesus circles the table. Peter resists for a moment, but Jesus knows well how to silence Peter. When he finishes his task, Jesus folds the towel and puts it back. He slips on his robe, walks back to the table and reclines. John 13:12–17 records his next words:

> "Do you understand what I have done for you?" he asked them. "You call me 'Teacher' and 'Lord,' and rightly so, for that is what I am. Now that I, your Lord and Teacher, have washed your feet, you also should wash one another's feet. I have set you an example that you should do as I have done for you. I tell you the truth, no servant is greater than his master, nor is a messenger greater than the one who sent him. Now that you know these things, you will be blessed if you do them."

Years later, the Apostle Paul summed up the example Jesus had left his followers with these words from Philippians 2:3–8 (emphasis added):

> Do nothing out of selfish ambition or vain conceit, but in humility consider others better than yourselves. Each of you should look not only to your own interests, but also to the interests of others. Your attitude should be the same as that of Christ Jesus: Who, being in very nature God, did not consider equality with God something to be grasped,

but made himself nothing, *taking the very nature of a servant*, being made in human likeness. And being found in appearance as a man, he humbled himself and became obedient to death—even death on a cross!

Jesus, our Lord and Teacher, *took the very nature of a servant*. Here Paul challenges us to a new perspective. He calls us not just to momentary emotional hype, but to a crisp, intellectual understanding of what Jesus models for us. He asks us to allow the Holy Spirit to renew our minds so that our reflex reaction at home, at work, at church, and in our community is humble service to God and people.

Paul underlined his own adoption of this mindset in the very first words of his letter to the Romans, where he introduced himself with these words: "Paul, a servant of Jesus Christ." It's as if he is saying, *Dear Friends, there are only two things you need to know about me. My name is Paul. And I am a servant of Jesus Christ.*

TAKE THE GAMBLE

Dr. Bilezikian continues to be a significant and much-appreciated mentor in my life, using not only his words but also his actions to point me to the servanthood model of Jesus. But back when I first sat under his teaching, I was a little hardheaded.

"This doesn't make sense," I said to him. "I don't see how it'll work."

"Just try it," he said.

Then he presented a challenge to me and to our little group of students and volunteer leaders.

He read us Jesus' words in Mark 8:34–35. "If anyone would come after me, he must deny himself and take up his cross and follow me. For whoever wants to save his life will lose it, but whoever loses his life for me and for the gospel will save it."

For whoever wants to save his life will lose it, but whoever loses his life for me and for the gospel will save it.

Then he challenged us to put those words to the test. "For six months," he said, "take the great gamble. Follow the model of Jesus with reckless abandon. Take advantage of every opportunity to serve—even if it seems like something insignificant.

"Be the one who opens the door for others. Choose the back seat of the car so your friend can sit in the front. Take out the garbage even though it's not usually your job. Volunteer to stack the chairs after the meeting. Take the arm of the elderly woman negotiating the stairs in the department store. Open your eyes. Keep your servant's towel handy. Monitor the condition of your heart, week to week. Then ask yourself: Am I gaining or losing?

"And if you want to," he said, "try it the other way. Every chance you have, put yourself in the center, be demanding, ask the world to revolve around you. Push your way to the front of the line. Disappear when it's time for the dirty work, the menial tasks. Bow low every morning in front of a full-length mirror. Then step back and honestly assess. Are you becoming closer to God and people or more isolated? Is your life fuller or emptier? Do you feel fulfilled or frustrated?

"Take the great gamble."

Those of us at the core of that little youth ministry, called Son City, decided to accept Dr. B's challenge. And at the end of six months, we had grown from a few students to hundreds. More importantly, our hearts for God and people had significantly enlarged.

We were all working harder than we'd ever imagined we would, but we were having a ball. We were discovering skills we didn't know we had. We felt energized. We were seeing kids' lives change. We were deepening our relationships with one another as we served together day after day.

Financially, we barely scraped together enough to live on—but we really didn't care. When someone's car broke down and they couldn't afford to repair it, we'd pool our money to fix it or pool our time to take them where they had to go.

We'd stay up late talking with students about their spiritual lives and get up early to plan programs; a short night's sleep seemed like a small sacrifice.

Jesus said, "I have come that you might have life in all its fullness." We were finding that fullness of life as we accepted Dr. B's challenge.

Three years later, Son City had grown to a thousand students on the simple foundation of faithful service to God and humble service to one another. The handful of leaders and the core of that youth ministry, who later made up the core of our church, had no seminary degrees, no experience in church-planting, no money, no facilities, and no maturity. But we had one gutsy Frenchman challenging us to accept the fundamental paradox of the Christian life: that following Jesus into radical servanthood is the sure pathway to fullness of life.

Sooner or later, everybody has to decide where to place their bets on life's great gamble. Where have you placed yours? On a self-centered lifestyle? Or on Jesus' model of servanthood? Where has it taken you?

If you're not pleased with your answer, grab a serving towel.

It'll be worth the gamble.

CHAPTER 4

The Great
Exchange

It is one of the most beautiful compensations of this life that no man can sincerely try to help another without helping himself.

RALPH WALDO EMERSON

In everything I did, I showed you that by this kind of hard work we must help the weak, remembering the words the Lord Jesus himself said: "It is more blessed to give than to receive."

ACTS 20:35

THE VILLAGE OF CASSANDRA IS NEARLY FOUR HOURS BY VAN from Santo Domingo, the capital city of the Dominican Republic. For most of the drive, ocean waves crash on one side of the road while mountains covered with lush vegetation rise up on the other. Stretches of dry pavement run past patches of banana and papaya trees, as well as fields of sugar cane and coffee. During the rainy season, mud slides frequently close the roads, but on this day the dust rises as Greg and his friends make their way from Santo Domingo, through the town of Barahona, to the little village where they plan to pour concrete roof headers and build walls.

During their week in Cassandra, Greg and his friends worked on two Habitat for Humanity houses—and also did a little work on their own hearts. "I saw kids wearing no clothes because they didn't have any, swimming in drainage ditches where people dump their garbage and human waste," said Greg. "I saw families living with no running water, and people and livestock crowded together in shacks where we wouldn't hang our garden tools."

Greg felt so overwhelmed by the crushing poverty that it took him several days to see the more subtle signs of hope. "I saw mothers working just as hard as fathers to build the houses, yet still taking time to kiss a cut knee or gently scold a child for wrongdoing. I saw a father's chest swell with pride when his five-year-old son picked up a bucket of mortar and carried it over to the men laying bricks. There was a man who couldn't work on his own house because he had just had surgery, but the community joined together and built his house anyway. I saw gratitude in the eyes of a man whose wife had died ten days before we started construction on his roof. I saw tolerance of our presence turn to laughter and hugs and heartfelt farewells when we left. I saw God melt prejudice in hearts that I thought would never change.

"I went down there intent on giving, but I received far more than I gave."

While Greg and his friends worked in Cassandra, another volunteer work crew stayed in the impoverished colonial area of Santo Domingo to renovate a new building for a thriving church that includes a high percentage of former prostitutes and drug addicts.

One of the men on that team was a fifty-year-old construction-equipment operator. His wife had left him a year-and-a-half earlier, and he was trying to rebuild his life, but it wasn't going well. One evening, halfway through the week, the team met to debrief their experience. In the middle of the meeting, this man broke down and cried. He said that for the last eighteen months he hadn't felt any purpose for living. But because he spoke Spanish, he had been able to talk with some of the addicts from the streets whose lives had been transformed through *Iglesia Comunitaria Cristiana*. After just three days of turning his attention away from his own life and focusing on others, he had begun to feel hope for the first time since his divorce.

"That's what happens on these trips," said his team leader. "When people extend themselves beyond their own concerns, their hearts always change."

These men took the great gamble and saw their hearts radically transformed. That's a common result of serving. One email writer expressed it like this:

> For me, the most potent effect of serving, regardless of the capacity in which I serve, is that it moves the focus of my heart off myself and onto others. Christ was the most "other-focused" person I know. I cannot imagine trying to walk with him without serving others. The more I serve, the more my heart changes.

Another volunteer wrote,

> The first time I worked in an inner-city children's ministry, I asked an eight-year-old boy if there were anything I could do for him. He punched me in the face. I felt like returning the gesture, but at that moment God dropped in my heart a compassion for hurting children that I never had before. That

moment changed my life forever. I believe that the compassion of God enters our hearts when we make ourselves available for service.

A BALM FOR INNER PAIN

While some people who offer a helping hand see their hearts transformed, others discover a balm for their own inner pain. Few people walk into a serving experience thinking, *I'm sure this will be a healing experience.* But many walk out realizing that a healing they hadn't expected has begun in their lives.

Jennifer, a young newlywed, made this discovery. While she and her husband dated, she got used to their long separations. But after eight months of "an awesome, God-centered marriage," he had to leave for a sixth-month tour with the Marine Corps in the middle of the California desert. The thought of his departure and absence hit Jennifer hard. In the months before and after his leaving, she prayed that God would help her endure the time alone.

Two months into the long separation, Jennifer felt that God was ignoring her, that he couldn't feel her depression. Then one day a neighbor told her about a fellow Marine and his wife who needed a place to live in the Chicago area. Because they anticipated just a two-month stay, they couldn't find a landlord to accept them.

Jennifer said a quick prayer and took the gamble. She told her neighbor that the couple could stay with her. "Since it was just me alone," she said, "I had plenty of room. Besides, I thought that maybe having someone around would cheer me up. The couple moved in the following week, and within hours I knew that God had answered my prayer in a miraculous way. They were a devoted Christian couple whose marriage gave me a sweet remembrance of my own. Through them, God sent me a clear message that if I keep him first in my mind I can handle anything. God called me to open my heart (and my home) and gave me hope and joy in return."

Ed too found healing as he served. Despite his many years as a Christian, his life had fallen apart. His wife had left him, he'd lost his job, he had just moved to the Midwest from California, and he was homeless and sleeping in his car.

One Thursday evening he made his way to our ministry to the homeless where one of the women serving food asked if he would like a Bible. Ed accepted the Bible but decided that as soon as he was able, he'd buy his own Bible and study materials.

After finding a temporary place to live, Ed visited our church bookstore. "I was walking around looking at all the resources, and I just started crying. I felt so brokenhearted. One of the women who worked there found me and started praying for me. Then she told me about a woman in the food service ministry named Peaches who loves to pray with people."

Ed went in search of Peaches, an African-American woman with a perpetual smile. "When she saw me walking toward her, she said, 'Oh my goodness, young man, come here.' Then she gave me a big hug and said, 'What do I need to pray for you about?'"

After praying for Ed, Peaches said, "Look, you are a young man. You wouldn't refuse to help an old lady would you?"

"No ma'am, of course not."

"Well then, come with me. I need help in the church kitchen. We have to make lunch and dinner for a whole lot of people who are meeting here today. I'll show you where the aprons are."

As Ed put on an apron, one of the chefs asked if he "knew how to sweat spinach."

"Yes sir. Do you do it with mushrooms and butter?"

Ed's experience as a chef in the military served him well. Day after day, whenever he wasn't at his job at Home Depot, Ed came back to volunteer in the food service ministry. "I just knew I needed to be here. Serving was working on my heart, healing me."

Ed had begun attending weekend and midweek services and decided to join the church. By the time of his interview for membership, he found the strength to tell his story for the first time: how he had become a Christian in 1973, had walked with God for a time but then turned away, and now was back. "I am here because I prayed to God to bring me back to him, no matter what it cost. I wanted the relationship with him that I had been created for. So I lost my home, my job, my wife—everything I had in California. I lost all the things that had drawn me away from God."

The person interviewing Ed told him that members were asked to serve at least one day a month. He laughed. "Don't worry, I'm here every day anyway. I love this place. People keep saying, 'Thanks for serving,' and I say, 'No, thanks for providing a place where I can serve.' I think that if God gives you a gift and you can't use it, you might as well dig a hole and jump in. Because serving is where the growing, the healing, begins. So now I just hold my hands out and say, 'Lord, just let me serve. Send me wherever you want me.'

"If somebody asks me if I have ever run sound equipment, I say, 'No, but I'd be willing to learn.' So they put me on a production team. 'Hey, Ed, have you worked with computers? We could use you over here.' So I serve with some folks who maintain the church computers. Wherever they ask, I go. I just enjoy it."

On Wednesday evening at 6:30, I see Ed in a church classroom that's been transformed into a café for high school students. I don't talk with him; he's busy making hazelnut lattes. But I know he's having a ball. And healing.

A VOLUNTEER EXCHANGE

Over the years I've observed a "volunteer exchange" that often works in the favor of the volunteer. I know this is a delicate subject, easily misunderstood. It's true we serve out of obedience and gratitude to Christ, to further the purposes of the Kingdom and for the good of those we serve, and it is crucial that we don't distort giving into a means of getting.

But the fact remains that the serving pathway—like any other road that leads to obedience—often brims over with rewards. It's Jesus' great paradox at work again: "Anyone who loses their life for my sake will find it." That doesn't mean serving is always pleasant or easy or immediately satisfying—sometimes the "loses their life" part really does feel like a loss, a painful, demanding loss—but serving in response to God's calling always ultimately changes our lives for the better.

The following emails highlight the variety of benefits that touch the lives of those who serve.

The healing of relationships

"My mother and I had been estranged for many years. She had kicked me out of the house and we were not talking. Then, on Thanksgiving Day 1981, she attempted suicide and ended up in a nursing home as a bilateral quadriplegic. She had no movement, couldn't talk, but there was some mental faculty.

"I was a brand new Christian. After church I would go to that little nursing home and try to help her. It started with a cup of water with one of those little kid 'bendy' straws. This one act took all the spiritual energy and courage I had, but I felt that somehow Jesus would be pleased if I served her as He would.

"This one act led to many others over the next three years—combing her hair, clipping her finger nails, shaving her legs, brushing her false teeth. It was very difficult for me to serve someone from whom I had been separated, but God used these acts to bring healing to me and to our relationship and to heat up my spiritual growth process. Serving my mother in this way opened a door so that I was able to lead her to faith in Christ. That ignited a passion for the Lord and the lost in my new Christian walk."

The opportunity to "give back" in gratitude for service you have received

"With our marriage on the rocks, my wife and I attended a whole year of *Marital Restoration* sessions. It probably saved our marriage, because I learned, among other things, about my contribution to our failing marriage, how to 'fight fair,' and how to pray with my wife. Every day I thank God, the *Marital Restoration* ministry, and my wonderful wife, because it worked.

"We were shocked when we were asked to become apprentice leaders, but felt honored to have this opportunity. We have been leading groups for troubled couples ever since. We are so thankful to God for this opportunity to give something back."

The chance to see God work in others the way he worked in you

"Four years ago I began serving at *Camp Paradise* work weeks. As a forty-nine-year-old man, I can think of better things to do than work like I'm on a chain gang from sunrise to sunset. Why do I do it? Because for the nine years prior to that, I attended more Father/Son and Father/Daughter camp sessions than I can count. And every time I attended one, God met me there. He touched my heart and softened my spirit.

"So I will dig, crawl, beg or do whatever it takes to be there and watch it happen to other men the same way it happened to me. If that doesn't light your spiritual fire, all I can say is, you must be wet wood!"

A new perspective on your own life

"Serving in the *Welcome Center* after the service has been a huge blessing. Often we answer general information questions. But sometimes people with deep hurts and needs stop by, looking for someone to listen and pray with them. During those moments, I truly feel the Holy Spirit providing me with words so I can respond with understanding. Whatever issues I am dealing with seem so inconsequential compared to the stories I have heard."

The discovery that formal serving encourages informal serving

"Serving keeps me in touch with why I am alive. My formal ministry of mentoring women in our church inspires me and impacts the informal moments of my life, extending the serving spirit to the drive home, the grocery stop along the way, the brief chat with my neighbor by the mailbox, and even to the guests who stay in our home. It is a joy-filled way to live, because it's the words of Jesus coming to life for me."

———•◆•———

On a radio talk show I recently heard that retired men who volunteer one day a week live two-and-a-half times longer than retired men who don't volunteer at all. Allan Luks, the author of *The Healing Power of Doing Good*, describes the very real physical benefits that accrue to those who engage in consistent, face-to-face service to others. Luks "makes it clear that when we persuade someone else to volunteer face to face, we are giving an enormous gift, much like a membership in a health club."[2] Helping others offers long-term health benefits, "including relief from back pain and headaches, lowered blood pressure and cholesterol, and curbed overeating and alcohol and drug abuse."[3]

Luks coined the term "helper's high" to describe the emotional well-being experienced by volunteers. Brain scientists at Emory University have discovered a scientific reason for the helper's high. Apparently, choosing to cooperate with others "activated an area of the brain rich in dopamine, the chemical that produces the pleasurable sensation activated by certain drugs and other addictive behaviors."[4] When people say that serving others "makes me feel good," their statement may have a more scientific basis than they realize.

I don't think this comes as a surprise to God.

Let me say it again: We serve because we have been served and because we follow a leader who models servant-hood. But why wouldn't the God who created us body, mind, and spirit call us to a lifestyle that strengthens our bodies, clears our minds, and soothes our spirits? God created us for a life of service—a life filled with rewards.

CHAPTER 5

What?
Me, a Priest?

JUST TO YANK MY CHAIN, A BUSINESSMAN FRIEND OF MINE introduces me to his golfing buddies as "my priest." His words elicit a shocked response for two reasons. First, I don't dress like their image of a priest. And second, my friend isn't close enough to any church to have a priest—or anything even vaguely resembling one.

In fact, my friend knows I'm not his priest, or anyone else's either. At least not according to his limited, stereotypical view of what a priest is. On the other hand, I most certainly am a priest. And chances are, so are you. For some of you reading this book, being a priest may be the furthest thing from your mind, but it's not far from God's mind.

THE JOB OF A PRIEST

Before the coming of Christ, the Holy Spirit operated through a select group of people called priests. Aaron, the brother of Moses, served as the first priest and his sons carried on the priesthood.

Old Testament priests mediated affairs between God and the people. To do anything religiously—pray, give a worship offering, confess their sins—the average person couldn't go directly to God; he or she had to go through a priest.

But Jesus' life and death turned the Old Testament religious system inside out. On what we now call the Day of Pentecost, when the first Christ-followers gathered in "the upper room," they heard the sound of a sudden, rushing wind. Then tongues of fire landed on everyone's head. I have no clue what those "tongues of fire" looked like, but they represented the coming of the Holy Spirit in full measure to the church. And the tongues sat not on the heads of a select few, but on *everybody's* head.

From that moment on, instead of a few, select priests filled and empowered by the Holy Spirit to act as go-betweens with God, suddenly every one of Jesus' followers became a priest.

This means that today we have direct access to God. We don't have to call a priest or a pastor every time we want to worship, pray, or confess our sins to God.

It also means that we become priests to one another. And what does a faithful priest do for his people? Prays for them. Encourages them. Watches over them. Confronts them. Grieves with those who grieve. Rejoices with those who rejoice. As a result, the people feel loved, nurtured, secure, and blessed.

Imagine a community in which every member takes his or her priesthood as seriously as did the priests of the Old Testament. A community like that would turn the world upside down!

According to Ephesians 4:11–12, God has uniquely equipped some of these priestly servants to train others how to serve (emphasis added): "It was he who gave some to be apostles, some to be prophets, some to be evangelists, and some to be pastors and teachers, *to prepare God's people for works of service*, so that the body of Christ may be built up."

Instead of the Old Testament temple system, we have congregations full of priests, with a few teachers, leaders, and pastors among the priesthood who are called to equip those priests for ministry. In most modern church settings, the "equipping servants" would be paid pastors and staff members. Those equipped to carry out the good works of ministry would be the "volunteers."

Throughout church history, whenever this plan has been implemented, the church has born great fruit. In such a situation, everybody wins.

- The equippers win each time they see God greatly use the volunteers they have recruited, loved, trained, and empowered.
- The volunteers win, because they get the thrill of moving from the spectator's seat to the playing field. They become instruments of healing, hope, and transformation in the hands of God.
- The surrounding community wins as it receives the service of a loving, unified, multigifted force for good.
- And of course, the Architect of the whole plan wins because God has the pleasure of seeing his children carry forward his grand purpose of fixing this broken world.

THE TRAIN JUMPS THE TRACKS

I'm not enough of a historian to define exactly how or when the church train jumped tracks, but jump it did. Although the early church started out with this beautiful concept of the priesthood of all believers—with every member an active minister and good works carried forth in all directions—during the last couple of centuries, most churches have retreated to the Old Testament model. Here's how it often plays out:

A group of a hundred people get together, decide to form a congregation, and "hire a minister." That's the terminology they use: hire a minister. Then they say to their new minister, "Okay, this is what we want you to do: Preach. Teach. Marry. Bury. Make hospital calls. Visit members. Counsel the confused. Evangelize the community. Raise money. Print the bulletins. Do announcements. Pray for the sick. Then, come year end, we'll get out our report cards and determine whether you have met our expectations. If you have, we'll sign you up for another year. If not, we'll hire someone else."

If the hired minister energetically throws himself into his multitude of tasks and the church starts to grow, the congregation might hire an associate pastor, an administrative pastor, or a youth pastor to take care of the programs and people beyond the senior minister's reach. But again, the congregation pays "the clergy" to do ministry.

So the church ends up with a few overworked professionals, paid by the tithes and offerings of the congregation to fulfill the whole gamut of priestly functions, while everybody else remains passive observers, their gifts and talents atrophying from disuse.

This is the most widely practiced ministry paradigm in existence today—and it doesn't have a shred of biblical support. Tragically, this approach has left many contemporary churches in shambles: weak, unorganized, and powerless. And unfortunately, it's a tough mindset to change.

Howard Snyder says in *Liberating the Church* that most church members "expect doctors to treat us, not to train us to treat others. We expect lawyers to give us expert advice, not to admit us to the secret fraternity of those who understand how the legal system works. Likewise, we want pastors to serve us, not to build and train us" to serve others.[5]

I think one of the reasons God made me somewhat thick-skinned is because for so many years I have had to absorb disapproval from people who want me to be like their doctor and their lawyer. They want me to perform my "priestly function" for them, never realizing that God is calling *them* to put on their own mantle of priestly responsibility.

"You're the priest," they protest, "not us." But the Bible replies, "Not true. If you're a Christ-follower, you're a priest."

It must break God's heart when people come to church with a consumer mindset, content to eat and run. "Serve me," they say. "Teach me. Pray for me. Fix my kids. Counsel my spouse. And if you don't do all of this up to my standards, I'll go down the street and see if another church will pay better attention to me." I've learned that you can't possibly build a God-honoring church with a congregation full of consumers.

Neither can you build a God-honoring church without teachers, leaders, and pastors committed to equipping. When those called to equip think of themselves as the only worthy "doers of ministry," when they peer down from their perch in the pulpit at their congregation, convinced that the Holy Spirit could not possibly work through the people seated in front of them, they are directly disobeying their calling and mandate from God.

I honestly don't know why some church leaders do this. I doubt it's due to scriptural ignorance. Perhaps they've never learned the skill of delegating responsibility. Or they don't know how to build a team. Maybe they feel insecure, afraid that if they share responsibility, another person's stature might eclipse their own in the congregation. Whatever the reason, they live as lonely, overworked clergymen, wearing themselves out doing the work of ministry, while bored potential volunteer ministers dutifully take their seats in the viewing stand week after week after week—and miss out on all the action.

I've heard many pastors say, "My people just won't get out of the spectator stands and serve."

And I have to ask, "Are you inspiring them to get out of the stands? Are you teaching regularly on the priesthood of believers? Have you reminded your people recently that they have the Holy Spirit in them? Have you made it clear that they don't have to go to seminary to make a huge difference in your church? Are they aware that they don't have to have theological credentials scribbled on a sheepskin in order to lead a small group, to serve communion, to teach, to make hospital calls, or even to start a new ministry in the church? Are you calling them to be part of the redemptive mission of God? Or are you presenting volunteerism as a duty, a drudgery they have to endure, like a parent asking a kid to take out the garbage?"

I remember an era at Willow when we had far too few volunteers. My staff colleagues would come to me and say, "Hey Bill, you've got to do something. We're trying to pull volunteers into our ministries, but it's not working. You've got to teach this stuff." So they got me all worked up, and

I finally stood up at our midweek service and said, "Okay, here's the deal. I'm going to teach about the priesthood of all believers. I'm not going to let up on it until we all get on board with it and we become a serving church. And I can outlast you!"

That was the beginning of a thirteen-week series. From the priesthood of believers, I moved to the concept of the Body of Christ in 1 Corinthians 12. According to that passage, the Body of Christ needs all its members—eyes, ears, nose, hands, feet—functioning properly in order to be fully alive. "Now you are the body of Christ," Paul tells us, "and each one of you is a part of it" (v. 27). Week after week I hammered home the truth that the body of Christ, the church, cannot do what it's called to do unless it becomes a community of interdependent, serving brothers and sisters. That's what it means to be priests and priestesses.

God used that series to add hundreds of new volunteers to our ministries. One church member told me recently, "It was almost twenty years ago, during week twelve of your marathon serving series, when I realized that God hadn't awakened me spiritually so I could just sit back and take in. He had called me to be a volunteer priest in this church. Thanks for not giving up on this message. Thanks for calling me into the game."

LIFT THE VISION

If we are going to be biblically functioning communities and maximize the potential of our churches, we need to lift the vision of volunteerism. Let me say it again. When those who are called to equip really do equip, and when volunteers show up to be equipped, trained, empowered, and entrusted with ministry, everybody wins—the equippers, those being equipped, the church, and the community. And God gets the glory because it was his incredible idea.

If you're reading this book and you're sitting in a church and not serving, step up! God has honored you by calling you to be a priest or priestess.

Accept the honor.

If you're reading this book and you're a church leader who is not equipping your people to serve, you are failing them. You can do better! You can decide to do better right now.

Rise to the challenge.

Imagine what could happen in your church and your community if every potential minister—priest, priestess, equipper, equipped—actually lived according to the biblical mandate. What an extraordinary power for good would be unleashed!

CHAPTER 6

Just
Jump In

IF I HAD TO SUM UP THE KEY TO FINDING THE PERFECT SERVING niche, I'd do it in one word: *experiment.*

That's not what I would have said twenty years ago, or even ten. Back then I would have said to start by figuring out your spiritual gift, that divinely empowered ability given to every Christ-follower that allows them to most effectively advance the purposes of God. Read 1 Corinthians 12, I would have suggested—and Romans 12, 1 Peter 4, and Ephesians 4. Then take a spiritual gift assessment test.

Learn and reflect, I would have said. Before you begin to serve anywhere, figure out how God has specially equipped you. Has he gifted you to lead, to teach, or to administrate? Are you especially good at extending mercy, encouragement, or hospitality? Do you feel uniquely empowered to communicate the Christian message to people far from God? Are you happiest when you can use your skills in craftsmanship or your creative talents in music, writing, visual arts? Do you feel fulfilled spiritually when you're organizing details related to a worthy cause or helping in practical ways behind the scenes? Are you known for being particularly wise, discerning, faith-filled, or generous?

First answer questions like these, I would have said, and then serve according to what you discover. I felt strongly about starting from the point of spiritual giftedness, because early in my ministry I discovered what happens when you don't.

A HARD LESSON

When Dr. B taught us about servanthood back in the youth ministry days, he also taught us about spiritual gifts. So as we served together we asked each other: *Who are you and what special talents and abilities do you bring to our corporate effort?* Along the way we encouraged one another to move toward the areas of ministry where we felt most effective and energized.

But planting a church for adults with no money, no facilities, and no paid staff was harder than we anticipated. We believed to our toes that God had called us to start a church to reach out to unchurched people and help them become fully devoted followers of Jesus Christ. But we had so few people and so much to do. The overwhelming demands on our time and talents sent us scrambling back to the concept of raw servanthood. We adopted the mantra, *Whatever It Takes.*

If something needed to be done, we didn't ask questions. We just put on the necessary hat and did it. We considered a match between a volunteer role and a person's giftedness an appreciated bonus, but it definitely wasn't our priority.

I preached, led the staff (all volunteers in the beginning), sang in two music groups at weekend services, discipled new believers, raised money, did strategic planning, visited people in the hospital, led a small group, and performed weddings and funerals. Everybody else in the core group served with the same intensity. When new believers joined the church, we challenged them to serve that way too—and they did. Our church wouldn't have lasted a year without that degree of commitment to doing "whatever it takes."

But after five years of serving with abandon, great people started flaming out. Men and women with pure hearts and deep devotion said, "I can't do this anymore. I'm exhausted." Others said, "I'm angry. What you're asking isn't reasonable." Some left the church so wounded that they had to get away to recover.

The way many of us had been living worked for a few years because of our youth and because we felt tremendously excited about starting a new adventure. But it was neither healthy nor sustainable.

We all had asked a single question—*What needs to be done?*—and we had answered enthusiastically with our actions. But we didn't ask these questions: *What are you good at? What energizes you?* And conversely: *What aren't you good at? What drains you?* We didn't think we had the luxury of asking such questions.

But as the decade of the '70s turned to the '80s, we realized there was more to faithful servanthood than just working harder. We had to work smarter. We had to move back toward the concept of spiritual gifts we had learned in the youth ministry.

We started teaching the concept of giftedness every way we could. We developed an in-depth spiritual gift assessment course called *Network*, which we taught throughout the year on Saturdays. We taught a nine-week series on spiritual gifts at our midweek services. We even came up with an abbreviated spiritual gift assessment that I used at our weekend services.

During the '80s, many people in our congregation discovered the exhilaration of serving in an area of perfect fit, where their personality, passions, and spiritual gifts all matched their volunteer role. But we ran into two problems.

First, the pendulum swung too far. An attempt to help people maximize their effectiveness without draining their energy slowly slid into an, "I can't serve until I find the perfect spot" mentality. It wasn't that people refused to serve in less-than-ideal circumstances. It was more that they thought they weren't supposed to; they thought they first had to "get it all figured out" so they could "do it all right." People knew their identity as servants and wanted to serve, but knowing how and where to serve had become a very complicated process.

Second, we had mistakenly assumed that the right assessment tool would assure people of discovering their God-given gifts. For some people it did work; they took the test, determined their spiritual gifts, and immediately started using them—a simple story with a happy ending. For many people, however, taking an assessment test was not enough. We discovered that the right assessment tool can be useful if a person has past serving experience to help inform their assessment. But for a complete rookie to Kingdom life, the approach often raises more questions than it answers.

We still believe that our ultimate goal is to serve in one's area of spiritual giftedness. But we have learned that spiritual gifts are less something we "figure out ahead of time" than something God reveals to us as we serve.

So here's what we recommend to potential volunteers these days. Embrace wholeheartedly your fundamental identity as a servant of Jesus Christ. Use whatever understanding you have of your personality, passions, areas of interests, talents, and preferences to guide you in a general serving direction. Look at the needs in your church and community. Then jump in with a willing heart and an open mind. Drape the servant's towel over your arm and get busy.

As you continue on the serving pathway and experience the joys of difference-making, you can then begin to study about spiritual gifts and ask God to reveal yours to you.

The key is to look at discovering, developing, and deploying your spiritual gift as a process. Don't worry about finding the perfect fit immediately. Give yourself permission to learn as you experiment.

A PARADIGM SHIFT

At our church, this concept of experimentation required a paradigm shift, not only for potential volunteers but also for staff and leaders. Most of our previous serving opportunities had required a commitment of at least three months—not at all conducive to experimentation!

Imagine having to sign a three-month lease on a car you are considering buying, versus having the freedom to take it on a forty-five minute test drive. So throughout all the ministries of the church we introduced the concept of the *First Serve*, one-time serving opportunities offered at a variety of times and tapping into a wide range of skills and areas of interest. Here's the *First Serve* mantra: *Come once and check it out. No strings attached.*

Some *First Serve* opportunities require registration ahead of time, but many allow potential volunteers to just show up. They are told exactly where to meet and assured that staff or experienced volunteers will greet them, help them get involved, and serve with them.

Consider just a few *First Serve* examples:

> Every Saturday morning at 7:00 a.m., volunteers are invited to help prepare the auditorium for the weekend services by setting up production equipment, moving props, and decorating the stage. Kids under twelve can serve if accompanied by an adult.

> On Saturdays from 8:30 a.m. to noon, people with carpentry skills can help with woodworking projects related to building maintenance or set construction.

> From 7:00 to 11:00 a.m. on Saturdays, volunteers help maintain the church HVAC system.

> Individuals interested in serving kids can show up ten minutes before any weekend service and take a forty-five minute tour throughout the children's ministry while it's in operation. They can observe teachers, small group leaders, and programming people, as well as learn about behind-the-scenes projects. Similar tours are available for junior high and high school ministries.

> First-time volunteers can sign up to clean bathrooms and empty trash during church services and conferences.

> Volunteers are invited to serve the junior high ministry by doing production set-up on Friday evening from 5:00–7:00 or on Saturday from 5:30 to 10:00 a.m.

Many new volunteers begin serving in the bookstore by bagging, duplicating tapes and CDs, or selling instant tapes after services.

Others help the sports outreach ministry by serving as a basketball scorekeeper on Tuesday evenings, or showing up at the sports ministry office during workday hours to do mailings or phone calls.

The food service ministry offers many opportunities at a variety of times, from preparing soups and sauces for the food court to creating table decorations for special events to serving food before and after services.

Adults are invited to greet students, distribute handouts, and help with other logistical needs at the weekly large group event for high schoolers.

Many one-time serving opportunities are available through our urban and suburban ministry partners. People can work in homeless shelters, attend racial bridge-building events at urban churches, prepare food and distribute clothing to street people, do painting and construction for inner-city ministries and general maintenance for a local camp for under-resourced children.

Throughout the church daily administrative opportunities are open to first-time volunteers.

FOUR IMPORTANT QUESTIONS

After each serving opportunity, we encourage volunteers to engage in a process of self-assessment by asking themselves a series of questions.

First, did the work feel meaningful? The answer to this question is purely subjective, but vitally important. For one person, it will feel deeply meaningful to stuff envelopes for a mailing about a leadership conference for pastors; they resonate completely with the goal (the conference) and with the people group involved (pastors), and they enjoy doing behind-the-scenes tasks. Another person may resonate with the conference idea, but if she hates doing repetitive tasks, she's not going to experience the work as meaningful. She may tell herself she *should* find it meaningful because of the worthiness of the goal, but she probably won't be motivated to show up again. Another person may discover that he really enjoys task-oriented work but would prefer to attach his tasks to serving senior citizens or children; for him, that would make the work seem far more meaningful.

Here's another important question: Was your emotional energy higher or lower after you served? Did you feel energized or drained? Serving can be exhausting physically but still deeply satisfying. If it proves emotionally draining, however, you're probably heading in the wrong direction. Introverted people often find people-intensive jobs, such as ushering, to be extremely draining, while extroverts thrive in the same setting. Some people feel energized by the chaos of a toddlers class while others leave the same situation needing a nap. A volunteer role that feels draining will not be sustainable.

Another important question (that many people feel guilty about asking) relates to the people with whom one is serving. Do you enjoy serving with them? Is there a comfortable relational dynamic on the serving team? Most people who timidly step off the spectator stand and onto the playing field feel motivated by the call to servanthood and to use their gifts for the good of others. But usually there's another dimension to their motivation, one they may not be conscious of. They want to get to know people. They want to discover like-minded brothers and sisters. They want their hearts touched by the power of community. If they don't sense the potential for that in a given serving opportunity, there's nothing wrong with continuing to experiment.

For some people, the relational component is more important than any other factor. Throughout the years, I've heard plenty of people say, "I wasn't sure if I wanted to serve in the bookstore"—or on the traffic team, or in production, or on the Monday night construction team—"but I kept going back because I loved the people I served with. Actually, I'd probably do any job to keep serving with them!" *Good for you*, we say. God made some of us to be so relational that finding the right serving team becomes one of the highest values in the serving experience.

The fourth issue for self-assessment is to look honestly at your schedule and the time frame for the serving opportunity. No matter how much you might enjoy a given opportunity, if it doesn't fit realistically into your schedule, you'll never be able to engage in it consistently.

Some people experiment with a *First Serve* and conclude immediately that they've discovered the perfect ministry fit; after serving street people in Chicago only one time, they are ready to make a once-a-month commitment. Others, however, discover that one dimension of a serving opportunity feels great while another part doesn't. So they use what they learned—both negative and positive—to inform their next experiment.

Let's say they take a children's ministry tour and resonate with the role of small group leader, but realize that a
roomful of noisy grade school kids drives them crazy. So for
their next *First Serve* they explore the role of small group
leader in the high school ministry.

If a person experiments with ten *First Serve* opportunities before they discover a "fit" that motivates them to make
a longer commitment, we think that's great; we cheer their
tenacity. How much better that they experiment and learn
rather than get stuck in a frustrating, unfulfilling, or draining situation that eventually sends them back to the bench.

Some people continue to experiment just because they
like the variety. For others, it's an invaluable opportunity
to invite God to clarify their calling, their gifts, and their
passion.

YOU NEVER KNOW

One thing that's always true about entering the adventure
of serving is that you never know what will happen.

When Jackie signed up to "meet a need" in the church
nursery, she didn't know she would spend the next twenty-
five years bouncing babies on her knee—and loving it.

When Tom decided to use his carpentry skills on Tuesday nights at church, he didn't know he would end up serving with other men in the church by helping single moms
with home repairs. "Fixing things" at church was a great first
step; but serving single moms allowed him to combine his
carpentry skills with his passion to minister to those in need.

When Phil met me for lunch and gave me feedback on
the church budget (that I had hastily scribbled on the back
of a paper napkin), he didn't know that he would end up

heading our church Finance Committee for the next two decades and find incredible satisfaction there.

When Karen began praying over the phone with people who called a crisis line she didn't know she would end up leading a team that meets faithfully every Thursday evening to pray for individual requests that are phoned in to the church throughout the week.

In 1974, when Jan agreed to keep track of administrative details for Son City, she didn't know her serving pathway would lead her from administration to doing drama skits—"Definitely *not* a great fit," she says—to leading small groups and eventually to a strategic and highly satisfying position on our church board of directors.

For these people, an initial experiment led, ultimately, to a perfect fit. Thus our motto:

Just Jump In!

Whether your first step puts you on the fast track to an ideal serving destination or begins a slow process of self-discovery, you will have embarked on the journey you were made for.

CHAPTER 7

Using Your Skills
to Find Your Passion

A RED BUICK REGAL PERCHES ON A HYDRAULIC LIFT. A Cornwell Tools storage unit—also red—dominates the back wall. The smell of motor oil permeates the pole barn where a volunteer leaders meeting is winding down. Only a few "housekeeping" details remain on the agenda.

"If you mix GM Red with Chrysler Orange, it's not going to work."

"What? There's not a full 10–30 out there? Sorry guys. I'll get right on that."

"You do not need to use a vice grip on the top of that drum to crank that baby down. Just hand tighten it."

Pete, the speaker, is our staff service manager for the *CARS* ministry: *Christian Auto Repairmen Serving*. The twenty or so team leaders he's addressing—themselves volunteers—lead close to ninety volunteer mechanics who repair twenty to twenty-five cars each week for needy people in our church and community.

The cars are donated by people from the church and the community, repaired and detailed by the CARS volunteers, then given to people who have fallen on hard times. Most of the recipients are single moms who can bring their cars back to the CARS volunteers for repairs and oil changes until they can assume the financial responsibility on their own.

For those being served, CARS ministry makes the difference between dependence on others for the daily needs of life and the independence that reliable transportation provides. It means the freedom to hold down a job, take their kids to the doctor, or go to the grocery store.

CARS provides a way for the volunteers to use their specialized skills to serve others in an extremely meaningful way. The majority of CARS volunteers are not certified mechanics. They're teachers and accountants and financial consultants who happen to love tinkering with cars.

"By vocation," says Jac, "I'm a white-shirt, dark-tie contract manager for a large healthcare provider. But I've always been a bit of a *gearhead*."

A lot of moms in our congregation and community feel grateful that more than a decade ago a bunch of gearheads decided to find a creative way to use what they were good at to help others.

And we've discovered that there are plenty of people gifted and willing to serve with their head under the hood of a car—especially when they get a taste of the rewards.

Jac says, "When a single mom drops off her car because it's the middle of the winter and the power window is broken and she can't close the window and can't afford to get it fixed, and two hours later she drives away with the window repaired and up—that is all the reward I need."

"When a car comes in and there's a baby seat in the back," says Pete, "you watch the guys in your team looking at the car seat and they just melt."

No money exchanges hands in the pole barn, but "we get paid every week," adds another volunteer. "One night a woman came in to pick up her car and she just kept saying—really loud so we could all hear—'thank you, thank you, thank you, thank you, thank you.' That's our repayment."

One Wednesday night at our midweek service I highlighted the CARS ministry during my message. After the service, a guy about six-foot three, 210 pounds approached me.

"I'm a brand new Christian or whatever you call it," he said. "I haven't been around here for long, but I've already caught on that I'm never going to speak or sing on the stage. And I probably wouldn't be good at visiting people in the hospital or teaching Sunday school. But can you give me the name of that guy who fixes cars? I'd be glad to show up every Monday night. I never knew I could help somebody by cranking wrenches."

But he can.

Maybe you could too.

WHAT MAKES YOU PASSIONATE?

As you've read various stories, illustrations, or emails in this book, you may have found yourself scanning some paragraphs with little interest while others moved you to tears or reminded you of a time when you volunteered in a similar way—or wanted to.

That energy flows from *passion*. A God-given passion—an area of intense interest—lies buried within each of us. One of the goals of volunteer experimentation is to discover that passion. Connecting our spiritual gift with an area of passion is the key to ultimate effectiveness and fulfillment in serving. It's also one of the keys to maintaining energy in serving. When you're serving in an area of passion, nobody has to fire you up to stay involved; you can't help but show up. It feels like recess, when the bell rings and you get to do your favorite thing.

Many people, like those serving in the CARS ministry, discover an area of passion as they look at the personal skills they enjoy using. This might be anything from professional skills to hobbies or recreation—from carpentry to gardening, computer programming to shooting hoops, doing research to organizing files.

Roberta, a hairdresser, found her passion through her professional skills. In the late '70s, she overheard a conversation between a client and another hairdresser in the salon where she worked. Month after month, this client, a new Christian, described her growing faith to the woman styling her hair. Roberta, listening in, became a Christian.

"From that time on," says Roberta, "I knew I was living for a higher purpose. I didn't want to invest the remaining years that God gave me in something that was just about vanity. In 1980 I bought my own salon. From the very beginning, I wanted that salon to be not just about hair, but about eternity. That affected how I treated my staff and my customers. It also planted in me a dream that God would someday use my salon in a unique way to serve women who desperately need encouragement."

Roberta's dream never died, but running her own business and raising a family kept her from actively pursuing it. Then she went through a divorce and ended up in a divorce-recovery workshop where she heard about our *Hairdresser's Ministry*.

Roberta began meeting with other professionals who love the hair industry, but who want to use their skills to minister to others. She heard moving stories from hairdressers who use their skills in nursing homes and centers for the severely disabled. Others described traveling to San Jose, Costa Rica, to teach hairdressing skills to women and girls trying to abandon a life of prostitution. She became convinced that if they could follow their dream, she could follow hers.

Now, several times each year, Roberta hosts a *Day of Beauty* at her salon. At each *Day of Beauty*, fifteen to twenty professional hairdressers from different salons each volunteer six weekend hours to style hair, apply makeup, and give manicures to women experiencing difficult times. The first *Day of Beauty* served women from a local ministry that provides transitional housing, vocational training, and counseling to single mothers who have become homeless.

Roberta and her hairdresser friends invited clients from their salons to donate clothes, shoes, and purses for the women served at that first event. "We had more clothes and accessories than we could handle. The women just cried while they tried on clothes. They couldn't believe they were getting all this stuff. Plus a new hairstyle."

The guests invited to the most recent *Day of Beauty* were teenage girls from a ministry for children whose parents are going through divorce. On another day, the hairdressers served pregnant teens.

A typical *Day of Beauty* starts with prayer, as the hairdressers meet to ask God to use their skills and their words to encourage the women they will be serving. Then they warmly greet the women and explain how they intend to "pamper them." (Hang with me here, guys.) Midway through the day, the women enjoy a beautiful luncheon donated by local businesses. Teresa, the volunteer who started the *Hairdresser's Ministry*, ends the day with a brief message based on Jeremiah 29:11–13:

> "For I know the plans I have for you," declares the LORD, "plans to prosper you and not to harm you, plans to give you hope and a future. Then you will call upon me and come and pray to me, and I will listen to you. You will seek me and find me when you seek me with all your heart."

"I love sharing those verses with the women," says Teresa. "We encourage them to turn to God for guidance when life gets difficult or when they feel alone. Because they know we truly care for them, they listen to what we say."

Roberta, who struggled to find value and a sense of confidence as she grew up, loves to watch the spirits of her invited clients lift as the day goes on. "I can't describe what it means to me to be able to share with these girls and women through touch, words, and service that they have value.

"It took over twenty years for my dream to come true. When it finally happened, it blew me away—and it still does. At the end of every *Day of Beauty*, all the hairdressers are in tears, grateful to be able to use the skills God has given us to make a real difference in women's lives."

The experiences of those in *CARS* and the *Hairdressers' Ministry* have inspired others in our church. A group of recreational and professional pilots, along with others who work in the aviation industry, decided to figure out a way to use their planes, their skills, and their contacts for Kingdom purposes.

At a recent *Aviation Ministry* meeting, Chuck, an aircraft broker, announced that he knew of an empty cargo plane flying to Johannesburg, South Africa. A Willow staff member who heard that announcement "just happened to know" about a garage full of computers waiting to be shipped to an African mission agency. Within two weeks, the computers were on the cargo plane, along with nine boxes of clothes and baby toys, headed for a Christian vocational training school in Johannesburg. And a group of grateful pilots and aviation professionals felt they had made a difference. "The last time computers were shipped to this mission," says Chuck, "fifteen South Africans were trained on how to use them and nine ended up getting jobs."

I never tire of seeing God orchestrate creative ministry plans through people who humbly make their skills available. Mike, another volunteer, is a gifted linguist. Every Sunday after one of our services, he teaches an idioms class for international attendees, most of whom are students from local universities. By highlighting idioms used in that morning's sermon, he helps increase the language skills of his students while clarifying the Word of God.

Here's one more skill-based story that I love. In 1980, Scott, a volunteer at Willow since the youth ministry days, decided to take his ski boat up to our church camp in Michigan and teach junior high students how to ski. "There was something about that age group," he says. "You could see it. When they succeeded at skiing, their confidence soared. Years later, I would have students tell me that learning to water ski at camp was a defining moment in their lives."

Volunteer-led from the beginning, the "water ski ministry" is still going strong. Our junior high students no longer attend the camp in Michigan, so on several Saturdays during the summer, volunteers with ski boats take groups of students to local private lakes where they offer a confidence-boosting experience that most of them would never otherwise have. As an added bonus, volunteers and students alike have a whole lot of fun.

TRYING SOMETHING DIFFERENT

Interestingly, some volunteers enjoy serving in a way very different from what they do in the marketplace.

A new Christian named Rich ran a billion-dollar food brokerage firm. For him, every day was filled with major financial decision-making and complex problem-solving. He did both extremely well, so I thought it made perfect sense to invite him to serve on our board of directors, where we desperately needed his level of business expertise. He felt more than happy to serve—but not on the board of directors. He didn't know what he wanted to do, but he knew he didn't want his volunteer experience to repeat his work life.

Rich eventually found his niche by establishing our benevolence board, using his problem-solving skills to help those in desperate financial need. He could have been making million-dollar, church-wide decisions impacting thousands of people, but he preferred to deal with the practical, daily needs of a single individual or family. I often saw him walking down the hallway at church with a single mom and her kids, who called him "Uncle Rich." He felt fulfilled and fruitful in his ministry, though it wasn't at all what his friends (and pastor!) expected of him.

The following email highlights one reason that some people seek to serve outside their area of professional expertise:

> During the week I do leveraged, buy-out deals in the marketplace. On Sundays, I serve in a room full of three-year-olds. The simplicity of teaching lessons—and changing occasional dirty diapers—keeps me centered when I start to get a big head from cutting hundred million dollar deals at work. Serving children keeps my heart soft and my feet on solid ground.

A volunteer in *Special Friends*, our ministry to disabled children and adults, expressed a similar motivation. I met him in a church classroom decorated with balloons and tinsel and colored lights, where twenty-five disabled kids and nearly that many volunteers laughed and played and sang their way through a Christmas party. Distinguished-looking and dressed in a dark suit, he said, "Every week I walk into *Special Friends* weighed down by concerns about business and customers and efficiency. Every week I leave *Special Friends* walking on air. This is the most important and fulfilling thing I do."

TRYING SOMETHING FAMILIAR

While many people find serving satisfaction by shedding their professional role, other volunteers love to serve God, the church, and other people with the skills they've spent ten, twenty, thirty years honing in the marketplace.

Randy is a corporate healthcare spokesperson. Dale is a national health care analyst. Becky is a human resource consultant, Rich a lawyer, and Rose a human resource generalist.

Dave heads up compensation for a major airline. What do they all have in common? They form a team of professionals who volunteer their time to guide the human resource department at Willow.

When rising health care costs threatened to force us to reallocate money budgeted for ministry, we asked Randy, a Willow member, to help our staff form a strategy for dealing with these mounting costs. Randy formed the above-mentioned team; some live locally and attend Willow, while others live in distant parts of the country and fly in quarterly to meet as a team.

In addition to scheduling and planning the meetings, Randy arranged for presidents of health care providers to present options to the group. His leadership allowed us to explore possibilities that would have been impossible if left only in the hands of our staff team. And the prayerful, spiritually sensitive perspective that these godly men and women brought to the professional challenge led to solutions that clearly reflect divine wisdom and intervention.

Randy and his team have devoted time, travel expenses, professional expertise, hundreds of emails and phone conversations, and behind-the-scenes prayer toward the human resources challenges at Willow. As they have done this, our staff team has moved into a lateral role, allowing Randy to truly guide the process.

Here's another example. John was a helicopter pilot and a political science instructor at the Naval Academy before earning his MBA from Harvard Business School. In his current professional role he is responsible for leading change and improving process efficiency in a major corporation. Wanting to "give something back" to God and to the church, he serves in the area of spiritual formation, using his skills of strategic thinking, leadership, teaching, and process improvement to help identify and address the major challenges to spiritual growth. "It has been a very blessed experience," he says, "that only encourages me to leverage the gifts God has given me in his service."

Dave, another young professional in our congregation, is an expert in organizational structure. When he wanted to get more involved in volunteer ministry, he joined several other business leaders in our church to help fund and organize *The Storehouse*, a ministry in downtown Chicago that provides affordable building materials for low-income housing. A ministry of World Vision, *The Storehouse* warehouses materials donated from manufacturing and supply companies, then makes them available to low-income housing agencies for a nominal handling fee.

Using his professional skills in volunteer ministry felt so fulfilling for Dave that he longs for others to have the same experience. "There are so many energetic, professionally skilled people wandering around churches, wanting to plug in, but the church isn't seeing what they have to offer. They're entrepreneurial, type-A people who are ready, willing, and capable of offering marketplace best-practices for the sake of ministry excellence, under the sovereign guidance of God."

Dave is right. It is time for church leaders to recognize the untapped expertise in our churches and to pursue strategic partnerships with professionals like Randy and John and Dave. I see two crucial aspects to such partnerships.

First, men and women with specialized, professional skills need to be tenacious in offering their services. Says

Dave, "You'll probably get turned away at first because church leaders won't understand what you're offering or how to use you. But keep working to help build understanding. And keep moving. If you don't find a serving opportunity in one area of ministry, seek one elsewhere. Don't give up."

Second, church leaders and staff need to remain open to sharing control. They need to allow volunteers into strategic levels of thinking and decision-making. For example, Tammy, our director of human resources, attends the volunteer team meetings, but clearly invites Randy to guide the group because he brings the necessary expertise. Thus, it truly is a partnership, one that has greatly benefited our church and satisfied the volunteers involved.

A COMMON SENSE APPROACH

The leadership of our church never set out to create ministries around the skills of auto mechanics or hairdressers or water ski fanatics or pilots. And we never thought that our human resource department would be significantly influenced by a team of volunteers. But we have always taken the common sense approach that ministry should flow from the gifts, interests, and skills of the people God has brought to our congregation.

In the mid-'70s when we started the youth ministry that birthed our church, we didn't set out to use drama and drums and dance—or any of the other "contemporary forms of communication" that seemed so shocking to many church people back then. But God had brought to us a bunch of kids with creative communication skills, so the outreach dimension of our ministry naturally reflected those gifts and passions.

The leadership of every local congregation must look at the biblical mandate for the church and pray that God will bring to them the balance of gifts necessary to create a whole and healthy body. But beyond that, I believe every local congregation should have a unique "flavor" based on the sometimes quirky mix of gifts, passions, and life experiences of its members.

I would not presume to offer a template for how to "shape" a local church. Every congregation needs to answer several key questions: Who has God brought to us? What are their unique contributions? How does the Spirit of God seem to be leading? What does common sense say?

I guarantee that whatever form of ministry or service a local congregation offers, someone in that congregation or in the community desperately needs to be served in just that way.

Thank God for the volunteers who choose to use the richness and variety of their gifts and passions to meet those needs.

CHAPTER 8

People-Driven Passion

CARRIE, AN ENGINEER FOR THE AIRLINES, IS YOUNG, BLONDE—and captivated by an inexplicable passion. "I have always loved Hispanic culture," she says. "I don't know why. I don't have a drop of Hispanic blood in me, though I wish I did!" Languages come easily to Carrie, so she studied and became fluent in Spanish.

When our church started *Casa de Luz* (House of Light), an alternate weekend service that provides teaching and worship in the Spanish language, Carrie, a gifted vocalist, began singing with the worship team. When she was asked to become the technical producer for *Casa de Luz*, she felt convinced that this was the purpose for which God had prepared her.

"I can't believe I have this opportunity to combine my gifts in music, language, leadership, and administration with my love for the Hispanic people. At *Casa de Luz* we have Puerto Ricans, Dominicans, Guatemalans, Venezuelans, Mexicans—people from all over Latin America. I believe God is calling us to join together as a unified force to minister to the growing Hispanic population in our community. I always wondered why I had this passion. Now I know!"

DRAWN TO A PEOPLE GROUP

While the people highlighted in the previous chapter have discovered their ideal ministry fit in connection with specific skills, others feel drawn primarily to a particular group of people. Read again Carrie's words: *I've always had a passion for the Hispanic culture. I don't know why.*

For people like Carrie, the passion that pushes them toward serving is a mystery, even to them. If you ask them where they'd like to serve, they're apt to begin their answer with: "Well, *for some reason*, I've always been interested in . . ."

They can't exactly describe that reason. But they can't deny the passion that draws them to serve a particular people group: infants, senior citizens, seekers, married couples, under-resourced families, internationals, teenage mothers, the disabled, or a particular cultural group. Like a river cascading down a mountainside, they find their interests and energy naturally flowing toward those people groups.

One Saturday morning, a van filled with adults left our church parking lot headed for downtown Chicago to help a Somali refugee family set up their first apartment in the U.S. None of them begrudged the fact that they would spend their day off with people they had never seen and with whom they didn't even share a common language.

They all talked at once: "We get to go downtown and help these people get settled. We get to take them food and clothing. We get to clean their apartment. Maybe we'll get to learn some words in their language." Their God-given passion for refugees turns a Saturday of serving into an exciting adventure.

Other people discover their passion as they respond to a particular area of need or a social issue: marital breakdown, grief, career challenges, addictions, abuse, injustice, poverty, racial division. Often their response to these issues is sparked by their own past experiences, often of pain.

Sharon felt devastated when her husband, a board member at our church, died suddenly. When she heard that a grief support ministry was starting, she attended the first workshop. The twenty people who attended with her had lost spouses, parents, siblings, and children. "People were experiencing so much pain," says Sharon. "The death of a loved one comes with many faces: a sudden trauma, a lengthy illness, accidents, the loss of an unborn child, suicide. But pain is pain. By the end of the first workshop, I knew the Lord had touched my heart for these people."

Sharon joined the leadership core of *Grief Support*, where she has now served for more than ten years. At the first workshop, a boom box provided music. Participants engaged in informal table discussions based on a book they read before coming to the workshop. Today, the boom box has been replaced by volunteer musicians, programmers, and sound technicians who show up every Monday to serve the grieving. Weekly teachers range from professional therapists to staff and pastors from the church. One hundred fifty people attended the most recent workshop. All of the fifteen table leaders were past participants who wanted to serve.

"What's most exciting," says Sharon, "is to watch people who come to us in pain, perhaps recommended by a friend, coworker, or past participant. Many of them have never attended a church, but they come and begin the important search for healing—and for God. Our hope is that these desperately hurting people will find a home for their hearts. The need is everywhere. We're just doing the small part we can to serve."

Rita, Laurel, and Gail started a different kind of support group: for families suffering from the impact of mental illness. Between the three of them, they had endured a son's severe bipolar disorder, a child's imprisonment due to mental illness, severe postpartum depression, and the suicide of a son and a brother. They knew they were not alone in their pain. Rita, a pastoral nurse at our church, knew very well that many families in our congregation and community deal with autism, clinical depression, schizophrenia, ADHD, and various anxiety disorders.

They met for two years, praying that God would enable them to minister to others. The result of their prayers was *Mental Health: It's a Family Affair*, a day-long seminar and a support group series designed to minister to those caring for loved ones who suffer from all forms and severity of mental illness. "You're not alone," they tell attendees. "Jesus Christ uses the storms in our lives to build bridges."

The theme Scripture for this ministry is 2 Samuel 22:17: "He reached down from on high and took hold of me; he drew me out of deep waters." That's what Rita, Laurel, and Gail have experienced, and what they now share with others.

I've received numerous emails telling similar stories of people turning their own pain into a healing balm for others. One woman writes:

> In 1999 I was in counseling and really a wreck. My counselor suggested that I join a support group for women at the church who had been sexually abused

and, reluctantly, I did. I grew tremendously and actually ended up becoming a leader. As a leader, I discovered that I had the spiritual gift of teaching.

Speaking the truth to other women who have been through the same things I've experienced has, in a way, redeemed a big part of my past. While I would never put the blame on God and say that he made me experience what I did so I could one day help other hurting people, I definitely believe that he took something horrible and has used it to benefit his Kingdom.

Another woman tells a remarkable ministry story that far exceeds anything she dreamed of:

About seven years ago, I saw an ad in the newspaper for mentors for teen mothers. Since I was only seventeen when my daughter was born, I thought this would be a way to give back to God and to thank him for the wonderful people he had sent into my life.

For the next two years I met with a group of teenage girls every week for fellowship and education. It was like having twenty-five teenage daughters all at once! I had no idea how attached I would become to them, how many desperate phone calls I would get in the middle of the night, and how helpless I would feel every time they made another mistake.

I helped them get shelter when their boyfriends beat them up. I bought them groceries when the paycheck just wouldn't stretch. I babysat their kids while they looked for jobs. But mostly, I just believed in them.

Because it was a government program, I could not openly share my faith. But it didn't take long for the girls to start asking questions about what I believed, why I was different, how I managed to stay married to the same man for so many years, and so on. I had many opportunities to share my life and testimony with them.

When our two years were up, some of the girls asked if we could start a Bible study. Wow! We met one night a week at my home, and my husband babysat all the kids in another room. Eventually some of the boyfriends started coming. I can't say everyone came to the Lord, or that it was easy. But it has been one of the most profound experiences of my life.

THE ELEMENT OF SURPRISE

While some people move into an area of service because of an undeniable passion, others sense God calling them to an area of service in which they think they have no interest. But when they choose to serve out of sheer obedience to God, they discover that he knows more about them than they know about themselves. That's exactly what happened in the following story.

Renetta describes herself as a city girl—"very, very, very city"—trendy, gas on the go all the time, working three jobs, self-sufficient—"like, please, I don't need anyone." She is tall and black and striking. Her nickname is Bubbles.

Renetta and her husband, Larry, a pharmacist, had been attending our church for many years and volunteering in *Service Ministries*—which includes counters, ushers, greeters, and offering collectors—when their service team decided to participate in a Saturday serving opportunity in an under-resourced neighborhood. With two busloads of folks from our suburban church, they traveled to Quinn Chapel, an African Methodist Episcopal church located on the border between the suburbs and the city.

"Everyone on the bus was white except Larry and me and Larry's brother, Garnett," says Renetta. "People were laughing and having a good time, but it was a nervous laughter. We were telling them not to worry, but that only helped to a certain point, because they didn't know what they were getting into. But when we got off the bus, Ruth, a woman from Quinn Chapel, hugged every single person like she had known them for ten years and told them how glad she was that they had come. That made a huge difference. Then the people from Quinn served us breakfast, a traditional African-American breakfast. Larry and Garnett and I were in seventh heaven, man. We had grits!"

For Renetta and Larry, it was a profound experience to have the people they served with at Willow join them at Quinn. Painting a chapel for one of our ministry partners was a worthy goal, but far more than a chapel got transformed that day. "They took us on a tour of the church, and there was so much African-American history there, pictures and artifacts. People started asking us questions. "Do you really do this? Did you know about that? Do you eat grits all the time?" They were truly curious about our world. For us, that was the beginning. They opened their eyes and we opened our eyes, and we all opened our hearts, and we became friends that day. It was an awesome experience."

Late that afternoon, on the bus heading back to Willow, Larry and Renetta were on a high—"It was a new day for us"—but they felt so exhausted they planned to head home immediately after the debriefing back at the church.

Only one thing stood in the way.

"All of a sudden, this Caucasian woman came into the room and literally blocked the doorway."

The woman felt determined to invite Larry, Renetta, and Garnett to a *Bridging the Racial Divide* discussion group, which met every other Saturday evening.

Despite the lingering euphoria from the afternoon, an intense small group experience surrounding racial issues had no place on their agenda. Evasively, they agreed to come sometime, maybe, if she would let them know before the next meeting.

"Well, actually we're meeting right now."

"We all got totally quiet," says Renetta, "but in the deep part of my heart, I knew we were going to say yes. We were dead tired, but it was obvious that our hearts were changing. We didn't necessarily feel forced to go, but kinda compelled."

In a large circle in a meeting room sat one black woman and eleven whites, plus the three newcomers. Despite their reluctance, Larry, Renetta, and Garnett spoke openly, convinced that any authentic bridging of the racial divide would come only by acknowledging that it existed and through a willingness to talk about uncomfortable issues.

But the evening did not go smoothly. When one woman in the group asked what "you people" prefer to be called, that set off the African Americans in the room. "Man, I was like *hold me back, hold me back*," said Renetta. They did hold themselves back on the outside, but inside, Larry, Renetta, and Garnett decided they had had enough. It wasn't the question that bothered them, but the phrase "you people."

"It has such a negative connotation," explains Renetta. "It's like you are grouping us together and setting us in a different section and saying, 'You belong over there and we belong over here, and if we extend the hand and bring you over here, then you can be accepted. Otherwise, just stay over there.' It has a big X of exclusion. To me it's one more way of isolating us, keeping us at arms' length."

In subsequent meetings, they discovered that the woman who asked the question meant no harm; she was genuinely trying to learn. But Renetta left the first meeting convinced there would be no subsequent meetings. "Why do I need to go back and talk about things that have hurt me, that have wounded me in my past? Why do I have to put that out on the table and have whites talk about it?

"With the trip to the church that day, our white friends had left their comfort zone and entered a world in which we already felt comfortable. For a moment, things had changed for us. But the *Bridging the Racial Divide* meeting brought everything back to reality. I was being asked to give a piece of myself that I hold very dear. A piece that within our culture there is no need to talk about, because we have all shared it.

"In spite of Larry, Garnett, and I growing up in very different parts of the country—Chicago, Oklahoma, Indiana—there's still a language between us that doesn't need to be spoken. We've all experienced the same kinds of indignities.

We understand it. But now you are asking me to sit in an environment where I am the foreigner, and not only am I supposed to feel excited about sitting with you, but you are asking me to open up a piece of me and give it to you. And why? What have you done that deserves that inner part of me? I'm all for the greater good of bridging the racial divide, but does that mean I have to expose and reveal who I am to you? That's a cold perspective, but it's reality."

So they didn't plan to go back—but "you know, God is bigger than us." The next week they returned. And then again, two weeks later.

"There was always something that we got out of it or that the other side got out of it. Hearing where some of the white members were coming from really opened our eyes. It helped us become more patient.

"We talked about funny things, like hair. 'No, I can't get my hair wet. You wash the oil out of your hair, I put oil in mine.' And we talked about some of the wounds in the marketplace and the community. 'You get up in the morning and go to an elite store in Barrington, and you get a "Good Morning." We get followed around the store.'

"Some of the people were fascinated because they had never heard the details of the everyday things that happen. They were under the opinion that things have changed. And they have changed physically—no one is making us slaves anymore—but there is still the mental anguish of going into situations and feeling so uncomfortable. You go to a restaurant to have dinner, you're the only black couple there, and you look around and see all these eyes staring at you."

It wasn't easy to stay in the group. Larry and Renetta continued to feel they were giving more than the whites, simply because there was so much about their history that the whites didn't understand and wanted to learn.

"Sometimes," says Renetta, "I just wanted to say, 'Don't try to make me your friend so you can study me!' That's how we felt, but we kept going."

When the group leader had a death in her family, she asked Renetta to lead the group in her absence. Renetta agreed, but just barely. In fact, in the car on the way to the meeting, Renetta made it clear to Larry that this was the last meeting she would attend. "We are going to go in there and do this, but then we are going to say, 'This is it.'"

But the evening went well.

Afterwards Larry said, "I have to tell you what I'm feeling in my heart. It's just me, and you may say this is just because I'm your husband. But I believe God is asking me to convey this to you: he needs you to do this. If you let him do this through you, he'll take it from there."

Reluctantly, Renetta led the next group meeting, and the next. "God was good, because when I would get in there and have that negative attitude, God would do something to spark my heart and make me want to stay. One step at a time."

Over the course of the next year, Renetta moved from being a substitute leader to a co-leader. The group continued to grow and eventually had to birth several new groups. Renetta and Larry both became group leaders, and Renetta ultimately became the coordinator of the entire *Bridging the Racial Divide* ministry.

Though Renetta continues to serve as a volunteer, neither her "unpaid" status nor her initial reluctance keep her from dreaming a big dream. "The dream God has given me," she says, "is beyond black and white. It's Hispanic, Indonesian, Asian, African, Native American, Lebanese, West Indies—all these cultures. They're all here. I don't know how God is going to do that, but I'm open to his call."

OPEN TO HIS CALL

Each story in this book is about someone being "open to his call." What would these people have missed had they not remained open? A challenge? An adventure? An opportunity? A calling? A purpose found in pain? A means of personal growth? A journey toward difference-making?

Each story also reminds us of the tremendous needs in our world—from racial reconciliation to comfort for the grieving, from training children to healing marriages, from serving the homeless to encouraging the disheartened. What needs would have gone unmet had the people in this chapter not let God work through their passion, their pain—even their reluctance—to touch others?

What passion might God be awakening in you? Is there a group of people or a social issue that you can't get out of your mind? Have you experienced an area of pain that softens your heart to others suffering similarly? Do you sense a spiritual nudge into an area of service that you never dreamed you'd pursue? Don't ignore what's going on in your heart right now. Let God speak to you. Listen. Then act. Take a step. Experiment.

Get into the action!

CHAPTER 9

Don't Forget to Ask

IF YOU ASK THE AVERAGE VOLUNTEER WHY HE OR SHE STARTED serving at a particular time in a particular place, most will shrug their shoulders and say, "Because someone asked me."

I believe that in churches all over the world there are people who love God, the church, and other people but have never crossed the line into intentional servanthood simply because no one has ever asked them to.

MANY WAYS OF ASKING

There are many ways of asking. Sometimes "the ask" comes in the form of a challenging sermon in which potential volunteers hear the call to get off the sidelines—and they realize that, for them, *it's time*. They may not know exactly how or where, but they need to begin the experimentation process.

Others may hear about a particular need that so obviously hits their area of passion that they can't *not* respond—and they know exactly how and where.

At our church, we work hard to make needs known. Each week we list serving opportunities in the printed program we hand out at our midweek services. On weekends, as people enter or exit the auditorium, we often play video clips highlighting various serving opportunities. We host ministry fairs and open houses. Last summer the CARS ministry held an open house at the pole barn where they work on battered vehicles. The open house featured classic cars owned by CARS volunteers and a genuine NASCAR race car donated by a friend of the CARS ministry. The goal of the open house was to attract potential volunteers. In one weekend, they signed up twenty-three new recruits!

But despite our efforts to publicly communicate needs and ask people to serve, by far the most effective ask is the personal one—and the more personal, the better. In fact, volunteers make the best volunteer recruiters.

An ad in a bulletin announcing the need for additional people to "adopt" flower beds for spring plantings may inspire a couple of garden geeks. But a fired-up volunteer who planted and maintained "that spectacular bed of purple petunias by the staff building" will be a far more effective recruiter. "It's just a few hours on Saturday. Come on. It's fun. And every time you drive on the campus, you'll know that you played a role in creating a beautiful, welcoming outdoor environment."

Volunteers make the best volunteer recruiters, but unless church leaders and volunteer coordinators model the value of asking, nobody will do it.

If I need to recruit a new board member, I always start with somebody I know. For years, the church has talked about "relational evangelism." We don't wander around the community and randomly pick out people to try to lead to Christ, because we know that we have far more credibility with people with whom we already have an established relationship. The same is true when it comes to recruiting volunteers.

If I am looking for a potential board member, I think about all the qualified people I know who aren't serving. If one of them strikes me as a possible candidate, I take the next step: I invite him or her to lunch and present the needs of our board. If they're not interested, that's fine. Perhaps just opening the discussion will prompt them to think about something else they would really like to do and I can help guide them in that direction.

CASTING THE VISION

The purpose of a one-on-one meeting is to cast the vision of the volunteer opportunity. This vision provides a compelling picture of the impact and the experience the potential volunteer would have if they decided to serve. Again, volunteers are the best vision-casters.

"Fred," a volunteer, might say to his friend, "I work in the children's ministry, and I want you to know something. The ninety minutes that I spend each weekend with the kids in my class is the highlight of my week. When I teach a kid from an unchurched family how to pray or tell a child from a broken home that God loves him, that's about as good as it gets for me. I was wondering if maybe you would like to come with me one time to see what God is doing in the children's ministry."

I believe it is generally unwise to ask a potential volunteer to make a long-term commitment up front; better just to invite him or her into the experimentation process. But I'm not suggesting we hold back in casting the vision! I never hesitate to tell potential board members how much I love

being on the board, what a great group of people I'm working with, the importance of what we do, and that I think
they'd love it too.

People deserve a clear and compelling vision.

If a member of our traffic team wants to recruit a friend
to help him, he doesn't say, "Hey Fred, would you be willing to help set up two hundred orange traffic cones at 6:00
a.m. on Sunday? It's a lousy job, but somebody has to do
it." He says, "Fred, I'm on the weekend traffic team. We
help create the initial impression for hundreds of seekers
who are visiting our church. We believe that we can enhance
the spiritual impact of the services by graciously greeting
people in the parking lot and efficiently guiding them into
parking places. Would you be willing to come and help create a great first impression?"

When our junior high director tries to draft people into
youth ministry, he doesn't say, "I know all junior high kids
have a frozen brain for three years and they dress weird and
they're generally obnoxious. But they need adult supervi-
sion. So would you bite the bullet and give me a little help?"
He says, "I've committed my life to a group of people who
are in the most crucial three-year period of life. MTV goes
after them. Most of the marketing for offbeat products and
destructive lifestyles is directed toward them. They haven't
yet developed the inner spine to make their own choices, so
they're very impressionable. If you want to make a huge
impact on vulnerable kids whose future hinges on the decisions they make today—if you really want to make a difference with your life!—then join our junior high ministry."

A vision like that almost makes *me* want to sign up for
junior high ministry (almost!).

A GOOD CASE STUDY

Once each week our high school ministry meets in a large group at our church. But on Sunday evenings, thirty to forty students from each local high school meet in private homes for hangout time, teaching, and small group discussions. One key to the success of the house groups is the small group leaders who lead the discussions and get personally involved in the lives of the students; they go to breakfast with them, attend their sporting events, get to know their friends, listen, talk, and pray with them.

Ruth, the point leader for one of the house groups, decided to recruit three twenty-something guys, Todd, Jimmy, and Michael, to be small group leaders. "Hey guys," she said. "We've got some excellent student leaders in our house group, but we desperately need some older, male leaders." She carefully explained the specific role of a small group leader. Then she added, "I know you guys—you're fun, energetic, cool, you've had life experiences the kids would relate to. You're just what we need. I think you guys could turn that whole school upside down—and you'd love doing it! So think and pray about. I'll get back to you."

For almost two months, the guys did think and pray about it. They started joking with one another about how they were going "to change the world." But the vision Ruth had cast was taking root on a deeper level: If they committed themselves to this ministry, maybe they really could make life different for a few high school kids. Maybe they could even help those kids grow in their faith so they could impact other kids in their school.

Ruth called to remind them that the invitation was still open. "We're still thinking about it," they said. She gave them a little more to think about by describing the positive contacts she had established with school administrators and staff and suggesting ways they might be able to build on those contacts. She also prayed—diligently and daily—that God would work in the hearts of these young men and that if he were truly calling them to high school ministry, that they would respond.

The vision sank deeper. The guys sat in church services on weekends, listening to sermons on "making your life count . . . using your gifts . . . taking risks . . . evangelism . . . discipleship . . . purpose," and they'd all be thinking the same thing: house group.

Ruth approached them again and invited them to have dinner with the other leaders and then visit the house group. They came. They discovered two things that night. First, that they really enjoyed the other leaders. And second, that the only way to get high school guys to discuss issues with any depth was to dive into the discussion themselves. "So, here's the action step I'm going to take this week," they said to the younger guys. "What step are you going to take?"

Two days later, Ruth met them for breakfast to debrief the house-group meeting: "How did you like it? Did it feel like a good fit? Could you relate to the kids? How do you see your involvement in the future? Is there any way I can help you explore this opportunity further?" (It didn't hurt that she paid for breakfast!)

It's no surprise to me that those three guys ended up becoming enthusiastic, effective small group leaders. Ruth did everything right. Through a mutual friend, Ruth knew the guys well enough to know they would, in fact, be great leaders for high school kids. And she knew them well enough to approach them personally.

So she asked. And asked. And every time she asked, she cast a little more of the vision. She convinced them that she was asking them to do something really important. Not only that, they would be good at it and love doing it.

Wisely, Ruth also offered them a specific job description. She didn't just say, "Hey, would you like to work with high school kids?" She asked them to serve as small group leaders for guys from a particular high school at a particular house group on a particular night of the week. Then she clearly stated their responsibilities. They wouldn't have to preach sermons, but they would have to lead discussion groups. They wouldn't have to spend every night of the week with students, but they would be expected to schedule breakfast meetings or occasional evening events to get to know their guys better.

Ruth knew that every potential volunteer needs to know exactly what they're being asked to do. A recruit's hesitance is often directly related to lack of information. People need to know their exact responsibilities, when they have to show up, who's going to be there, and how much time it's going to take. They cannot say yes to a bunch of unknowns. And they need assurance that the request being made of them is reasonable.

Back to Ruth. When the guys did express interest in the ministry, she invited them to have dinner with the other small group leaders. She knew that if they were going to spend a minimum of one night each week serving with her team, they had all better find out right away if they had a relational connection on which they could build.

DON'T NEGLECT THE DEBRIEF

After the first house group, Ruth followed through with the most neglected—and arguably the most important—part of the recruiting process: the debrief. Too often the recruiting pattern goes like this: You ask. You finally get somebody to show up. Then you cross your fingers and hope they liked it and that they'll come back.

Why not sit down with the fresh recruit and discuss what the serving experience was like for them? We need to remember that recruiting volunteers isn't just about fitting people into slots and getting our ministry needs met. It's about giving people permission to experiment and learn. It's about guiding a person along a pathway of spiritual growth. It's about helping people discover their spiritual gifts and passions.

So we need to debrief. If volunteers say they loved every minute of the experience, we can just cheer them on and encourage them to continue. If they express reservations about going back, we need to find out why.

Was it a breakdown in the system? Did the volunteer leader not show up on time? Did the volunteer end up working in isolation rather than with a team? Was the necessary training neglected?

Or was there a personal discovery? Did they realize they don't like toddlers? They don't enjoy administrative tasks? They can't handle having to show up at 7:00 a.m. on Saturday?

Could the job be tweaked to make it fit better? What would their fantasy role look like? Is there a way to modify this volunteer role to create a win-win situation?

One of our board members who had served faithfully for many years learned that he had to relocate to another part of the country or agree to travel Monday through Friday nearly every week. Either way, this man would have to give up his board position—or so he assumed. But when I asked him if there were some way we could adjust his board involvement to make his continued service workable, he came up with an option we found easy to implement. It required only a slight shift in responsibility and time commitment.

Later he sent me a thank-you letter. "It made a huge statement to me," he wrote, "that you valued my contribution as a board member enough to custom fit the position to my new circumstances." He needn't have thanked me. Making that adjustment allowed me to retain the services of a valuable volunteer. After several years, his vocational situation again changed, and he was able to resume his previous level of board involvement.

THREE KEY LESSONS

A great volunteer culture never happens by accident. It always requires a major investment by church staff. I want to end this chapter with three lessons that church leaders need to keep in mind.

1. A new volunteer is a fragile volunteer

A long-time volunteer can handle an occasional volunteer mishap. But a new volunteer is extremely vulnerable to discouragement and disillusionment. And that first volunteer experience may well determine that person's attitude toward ministry for the rest of his or her life.

We've all seen it: A fresh volunteer steps up to serve and a careless church leader stuffs her into a position outside her giftedness, interest, or skill. The leader doesn't uphold the value of experimenting by providing an easy exit route—"Hey, if this doesn't work for you, we'll find another option that does"—so the volunteer shows up faithfully for a year, all the while feeling ineffective, unfulfilled, and drained. She works hard but never excels. When she tries to quit, the pastor or ministry director says, "Come on. Be committed. Don't give up. Don't let God down."

But often it isn't a commitment problem. When people get out of the spectator stands and put on a serving uniform, it's usually because God has touched their hearts and they want to make a difference in the Kingdom. But a serving experience that feels consistently defeating can push people to the point where they'll accept the guilt of quitting, climb back up on the spectator's stand, cross their arms, and dare another church leader to get them onto the serving field.

I've often heard words like this: "Bill, I'd like to serve, but I can't right now. My wife and I need to take a break. For ten years we led the small group ministry at our former church. But we put in too many hours, we never received the training we needed, and our supervisor didn't respond to our requests for help. We're exhausted. We can't do it anymore. We need to heal up from that experience." How sad.

Sometimes our church needs to become a hospital for wounded servants from other churches—and sometimes for those from our own church. We've made plenty of mistakes that have hurt people, and we need to allow them the time to heal.

How can we avoid that? Once again, the answer is embarrassingly simple. Ask. Write a note. Call. Take a new volunteer out to lunch and ask a few basic assessment questions: "How did that feel? Did it breathe life into you? Do you look forward to doing it again?" And along the way, check in with veteran volunteers: "How's it going? Are you still satisfied in your position? Are there any adjustments we need to make?"

2. The easiest way to defeat a volunteer is to waste his or her time

Volunteer coordinators, in particular, need to keep this lesson in mind.

Here's how it happens: A pastor teaches about serving, creatively communicates needs, and extends personal invitations. People sign up to serve. In best-case scenarios, they're even directed into their areas of giftedness and passion.

So the volunteer leaves work early and gets a babysitter, drives forty-five minutes, and shows up ready to serve—and then discovers that he isn't even needed. There's simply not enough work; the project could easily have been completed without him. Or it's all busy work. The specific skills he offered to bring aren't even required for this job. Or worse yet, the project isn't ready on time. The volunteer stands around for twenty minutes waiting for someone to show up with the letters he's supposed to stuff into the envelopes. Wasting a volunteer's time is the best way to assure that he'll never show up again.

On the other hand, an equal danger exists of loading too much responsibility on a volunteer. A young married couple offers to help the pastor with the youth group and three weeks later the pastor says, "It's all yours. You are now the youth sponsors. These twenty-five kids belong to you!"

If the responsibility given to volunteers doesn't match their stage in life, their energy, or their level of skill, it's only a matter of time before they quit. And it's not their fault. It is the responsibility of church leaders and staff to help volunteers discover an appropriate window of responsibility in which they are neither underutilized nor overwhelmed.

How do you find this precise spot on the serving continuum? Again, debrief. Ask. Listen. Get to know your volunteer. Care. Remember that you're not just filling a serving slot to meet a need; you're guiding a willing-hearted Christ-follower along a pathway toward a fulfilling, fruitful lifestyle of servanthood.

3. Servants need to be reminded—constantly—that what they're doing is not in vain

Volunteers should be reminded, again and again, that they're valued; that what they're doing is part of the redemptive drama that's been going on throughout human history; that the role they are playing is not insignificant; that God treasures every task they perform, every hour of service they render.

Matthew 6:4 says, "Your Father, who sees what is done in secret, will reward you." Not a single act of service done in the name of Christ goes unnoticed or unrewarded. No kind word, no encouraging smile is ever lost. Every deed of charity, every gift of mercy, every letter of inspiration, every hour devoted to serving your spouse, your kids, your parents, your employer, your ministry director, a stranger on the street—every single action of servanthood gets noticed and will be rewarded by God. We owe it to people to remind them of that.

First Corinthians 15:58 says, "Be steadfast, immovable, abounding in the work of the Lord, knowing that your work is not in vain." That's my life verse. When I get discouraged or weary, I say it a little differently: *It is never in vain, there is nothing I do in the name of Christ that is ever in vain.* Though the visibility of my life offers a certain level of reward, on plenty of days I leave my office thinking that I disappointed more people than I encouraged, or that my leadership or teaching felt ineffective. I have to remind myself that at least I showed up, I tried, and God saw that. And that can't be taken away from me.

If I have to go through that kind of mental discipline to keep myself motivated and faithful, what about the person who stands out in subzero weather directing cars into parking places or cleans up dirty tables in the food court or pushes a vacuum around the auditorium on Saturday morning? They too need to be reminded that God sees and values what they do. That there are witnesses in heaven cheering them on. That the impact of their service will ripple throughout eternity.

Volunteers need to be reminded that *they're not crazy.* I know how much I appreciate it when I'm affirmed and told that what I'm doing is important. I believe that most people feel the same way. We all carry the same doubts inside. We need to create a culture of encouragement by taking the time to look each other in the eye and remind each other that what we're doing matters. *God sees it, and for what it's worth, I see it too. Your faithfulness matters. Your gifts matter.*

It doesn't take many words to encourage someone. You can walk by somebody in the hallway, put your hand on their shoulder, and say one sentence: *I'm glad you're on the team . . . This ministry wouldn't be the same without you . . . Thank God for what you're doing.*

One Friday evening I was speaking at a new-building dedication service for a church in another state. On the way to the auditorium I walked past the nursery and saw a woman with a baby in each arm. I felt preoccupied, digging my notes out of my briefcase, but I received a clear nudge— I thought from the Holy Spirit—to stop and thank the woman for serving in the nursery.

"Ma'am," I said, "I know you'd probably rather be in the auditorium with the rest of your church, celebrating the opening of your new building. But here you are with a baby in each arm. I commend you for your spirit of servanthood and your willingness to make it possible for other families to enjoy the church service tonight. Way to go!"

Later, I received a note from that woman. "Dear Pastor," she wrote. "I've been working in church nurseries for twenty-two years. When you stopped and talked to me, that was the first time I've ever been thanked by a church leader."

I read that and I thought, *Why do we do this to volunteers? Why does saying thank you to the hidden heroes of the local church go to the bottom of our list?*

If you're a faithful, consistent, humble volunteer in your church or community, I want to thank you right now for showing up and making a difference. Your gifts matter. Your passion matters. Your official works of service matter. Your unseen acts of kindness matter.

Your labor is not in vain! Way to go!

CHAPTER 10

Over the Long Haul

Let us not become weary in doing good, for at the proper time
we will reap a harvest if we do not give up. Therefore, as we have
opportunity, let us do good to all people.

GALATIANS 6:9–10

It would be hard to find a lousier restaurant than
Tasty's Diner. The service was lousy, the food was lousy, the
décor was lousy, the lighting was lousy. Everything about it
was lousy, except for one thing: it was open all night long.

In the early days of Son City, when we all worked so
hard as volunteers that every week we felt tempted to quit,
we would meet at *Tasty's Diner* after the Thursday night
outreach event. Sitting in a corner booth with vinyl uphol-
stery, we would review what we had done that night. Usually we began by complaining. We started the meeting fifteen
minutes late, again. The drama kid dropped a crucial line.
One of the lights on the lighting tree exploded right during
the message.

We'd complain for awhile, and then we'd start laughing.
We knew we either had to laugh or cry, and we chose the
former.

By the time the food got served we would have mellowed out, and we'd start sharing stories about that night's significant conversations with kids. Gradually we'd slide into talking about our own lives, about how we were struggling or growing or how it was going with family or friends. As the hands of the clock moved from p.m. to a.m., our conversation deepened. Eventually someone would glance at their watch and gasp, our signal that the time had come to leave. We would feel sorry to end the conversation but so tired we could barely make it to our cars.

On our way through the parking lot, one by one we'd say, "Hey, see ya next week."

Of course, we all signed up for another week. We loved each other and loved to serve together. The community we shared in the glow of that dingy restaurant's fluorescent lights provided one of our major paybacks for the blood, sweat, and tears we poured into ministry. We loved God and wanted to serve the students in his name. And the community that surrounded our serving helped to renew our energy so we could keep on doing it.

AND THE BEAT GOES ON

Linda was a vocalist in the Son City band during those beginning years, and she has never stopped singing. A school teacher by vocation, she is still faithfully serving our congregation with her gift of music. For almost thirty years, she's been showing up for midweek, weekend, and holiday services—and the thousands of rehearsals those have required—to serve as a backup singer, humbly leading our congregation in worship or helping to create a programming "moment" that touches people's souls. For many of those years, she has also been a signer for the deaf, interpreting songs and drama during midweek and weekend services.

Laurie was seventeen when she started serving in Son City as a team leader for her high school. At age twenty-two, she became an elder in our church. For the next twenty-five years, while holding a management position in a commercial real estate company, she attended literally hundreds of late-night elder meetings to make major spiritual decisions on behalf of our church, pray for the sick, handle church discipline, and provide guidance to our staff. Now retired from "eldering," Laurie is pursuing a new passion. With the same fervor that she poured into helping to lead our church, she is now assisting African refugees as they resettle in the Chicago area.

Quigley has also served our church faithfully for almost three decades. He had been a Christian only for a year before volunteering to help find land on which our new church could build. We were meeting in a movie theater and looked forward to a facility where we didn't have to deal with X-rated marquees and hold our children's ministry in a dirty lobby that smelled like stale popcorn. Quig discovered that his doctor owned a piece of property at the corner of Barrington and Algonquin roads. We moved into a building on that land in 1981, and we're still there. Quig also has been the chairman of our board of directors since it started; he's chaired every meeting we've ever had. About his role as volunteer he says, "Thanks for giving me the most important, fulfilling role of my life. I plan to keep doing this until they have to carry me out in a box!"

These people have committed themselves to being lifelong volunteers in the Kingdom of God. According to the Bible, that should be the norm. Jesus taught that servanthood isn't about giving it a shot for two years and then losing interest, or about serving with abandon for five years and then flaming out. Servanthood is the primary calling on our lives.

But working consistently as a volunteer in the church is hard. So we need to understand what sustains volunteer energy over the long haul.

KEYS TO STICKING WITH IT

The first key is something that we discussed in previous chapters: to gradually align oneself closer and closer to authentic areas of passion and spiritual giftedness. The second way is to serve within the context of community.

In the initial stages of serving, the "helper's high" can feel so strong it's almost seductive. *Wow, this enriches my life! This makes me feel so good!* But anyone who serves consistently knows that the euphoria probably won't last. At a certain point, you realize that serving isn't about you. It is about God and about the needs of those you are called to serve. Sometimes meeting those needs feels good; sometimes it's just plain, flat, demanding work.

I walk around our church and see hundreds of volunteers showing up week after week to do thankless, repetitive tasks. I see others carrying levels of responsibility that probably exceed what they do in their marketplace professions. I see some give up "billable" hours at work so they will have more time to serve for free at church. I see others who—literally—volunteer full time.

I often wonder how they keep doing it. I know they're human. I know that sometimes they get beat up and discouraged. I know that some of them probably haven't discovered their perfect "fit," in terms of gifts and passion, so their serving is harder than it ought to be. How do they maintain the energy to keep showing up?

Then I walk through the atrium area of our church and see groups meeting around tables before or after they serve. They open up their lives to each other, laughing and praying and crying with each other.

Then I remember *Tasty's Diner*.

I've said many times in recent years that I have two goals for the rest of my life. First, I want to do the work God asks me to do. I've never known joy outside of pursuing God's calling on my life. Whenever I've wandered even five degrees off that course, I've lost the sense of God's smile that I can't live without.

Second, I want to do the work God calls me to do in community with people I love. While most of the serving circles in which I now sit are not volunteer circles, the same principle applies.

At a recent management team meeting, I experienced both the highs and lows of community. Some people shared hilarious accounts of joy-filled family moments that had occurred during the week; but others spoke through tears. Afterwards I sat at my desk and thought, *Nothing beats being invited into the joys and sorrow of the people with whom I serve and to have them join in the joys and sorrows of my life. I don't ever want to do God's work apart from community.*

I know that sounds self-serving. The truth is, if God called me to serve in the total isolation of a dark cave, I hope I'd do it. And of course, for all of us some aspects of our service require a solitary focus. But I don't believe God's design calls us to be solo servants.

If we want a model of this, we need only look as far as Jesus. While he spent time in solitary prayer and reflection, he didn't walk around teaching large crowds and sleeping on mountainsides alone. During the majority of his public ministry, he served in a community of twelve, and even more intimately, in the inner circle of three.

At our church, we've driven this stake in the ground. We are committed to offering volunteers exactly what we believe God had in mind: the opportunity to serve faithfully in the context of a community so rich that it touches their hearts, gives them joy, and energizes them for continuing service.

We didn't always do this. For example, we used to have solitary volunteers mow the grass on the church property. A guy would show up, drag the mower out of the pole barn, fire it up, mow for a few hours, then go home. He had no contact with anybody—and we wondered why our mowers had low motivation and high turnover! When we finally bought additional mowers and created a mowing team, motivation and longevity both shot sky high. Here's how one email writer describes the power of working on a team:

> I want to tell you about working on the *Grounds Team*. The team met on Saturdays from 7:00 a.m. to 3:00 p.m., with a break for coffee at 10:00 and lunch at noon. I don't know which I looked forward to more, the breaks or the work. They were equally fulfilling. During the morning break, we'd sit in a circle and have juice or coffee, with donuts or coffee cake. We'd go around the circle, each of us talking for five or six minutes about personal things. We could share most anything during those times. Sometimes heavy stuff, sometimes lighter stuff. We got to

know each other pretty well. There's something special about being assigned a task and then joining hands to pray for a productive day and safety . . .

I know the relationships that developed in that group were no accident. I always thought that when Dan, the leader, assigned us projects, like laying sod or planting shrubs or tulip bulbs, he probably thought, *Now, who would Gary benefit from working with today?* In that group, I learned what community was all about.

I'm in the retail business and have to work on Saturdays now, so I'm serving in a different ministry, but every Saturday morning on my way to work I drive past the church and remember the days spent on campus pruning, racking, planting, and coming alongside a fellow Christian with one common desire . . . to serve the Lord . . . together.

Doreen wrote the following about her experience of serving in community:

I've been serving in the children's ministry for over twenty years. I've had incredible experiences, not only with the children but also with the teams I've served with. My current team is as much family to me as my biological family. Almost every Saturday evening after working with the kids we go out to eat and talk until we close down the restaurant. We've helped each other move, gone to each other's weddings and taken each other to the airport.

We also sit together at most services. I know they would miss me if I didn't show up, so it's a form of accountability. The verse about iron sharpening iron really describes us; we've all grown in our faith as a result of doing life together.

This church can feel pretty big. I've overcome that by getting connected in serving.

HOW TO KEEP VOLUNTEERS MOTIVATED

Community clearly plays a huge role in sustaining servant-hood. In the remainder of this chapter, I want to mention several additional factors that keep servants motivated.

1. Serving energy builds as we see transformation in the lives of those we serve

Paul writes to the flourishing church in Thessalonica, "For now we really live, since you are standing firm in the Lord" (1 Thessalonians 3:8). He's describing the spiritual rush servants enjoy when they see people they've served growing spiritually and living God-empowered lives.

The Apostle John writes, "I have no greater joy than to hear that my children are walking in the truth" (3 John 4). He's talking about spiritual children, people he has served and in whom he's invested.

Every dedicated servant of God I know has been through some wilderness experience in serving others. A small group he led fell apart. A person she mentored returned to a destructive lifestyle. "What's the use?" they ask. "People don't care. They don't change. My contribution means nothing. I'm wasting my time."

But they keep on loving and praying and teaching and offering tangible acts of service, and some of that effort touches hearts and produces lasting change. At church or at the grocery store or in the neighborhood park they run into someone who says, "Hey, I want you to know that the way you lived out the spirit of Christ by bringing me meals when I was sick made me want to be a Christ-follower too." Or "When you shared the story of your healing process at our support group, you gave me hope to keep persevering through my own grief. Thank you for your honesty." Or "You may not remember me. But you were my son's small group leader in junior high. He's in college now and he's still walking with the Lord. Thanks for investing in him."

Suddenly these servants understand what Paul meant when he said that impacting a person spiritually made him "really live."

Consider an email I received from a young man who has served for ten years in our basketball ministry, which reaches out to people in our community.

> The season that just ended has been the most rewarding one I've had. Four years ago I inherited a basketball team of younger guys. Connecting with them was a bit difficult at first because I didn't know any of them, but slowly we bridged the gap. Now, we're no longer "just" a basketball team. We're a group of guys who love to be with each other, on and off the court. Others have seen how much fun we have together and have wanted to join our "Merry Band" of brothers. It has been rewarding to realize that other people can see a dimension of the Christian life through players who are running and shooting and sweating on a hardwood floor.
>
> But what made this season such a highlight was that one of my team members became a Christian . . .

and I helped lead him along that path! What an honor to be able to tell someone that I had gotten to know and love for four years that there was a party in heaven in his honor. It was so humbling. With all the mistakes I make, the Holy Spirit used me to reach a lost soul and bring him into the family of God. This is probably the most amazing aspect of being a Christ follower ... how God can take an immensely flawed individual and use his willingness of heart and his gifts to reach other flawed individuals. I can tell you from the bottom of my heart, there is nothing more rewarding for me than what happened on my basketball team this year.

One way that volunteers can join in the celebration of God's transformation of human lives is through baptism services. I believe that every person guided toward faith through the ministry of a church is a testimony to the contribution of every volunteer.

Perhaps at some moment the words offered by one of our teachers "clicked" and the hearer knew that the message of God's grace was for him. But that message would never have been heard without the production volunteers who show up early to set up sets and technical equipment while the rest of us sleep. And the message may not have settled in the hearer's heart without the song sung by the volunteer vocalist, who prays every time she sings that God will use her lyrics and her melody to break through emotional and spiritual barriers. And the volunteers who vacuum the auditorium every Saturday morning know that they too have been a part of every spiritual decision made in that room.

Every baptism service celebrates a transformed life, but it also celebrates the Body of Christ. It celebrates the hands and feet and eyes and ears and hearts that work together according to God's design. And the little surge of energy that fills the soul of every volunteer watching a baptism is a gift from the Holy Spirit who says, "You had a part in the transformation of a human life. Own that. Revel in the knowledge of being used for God's purposes. Be encouraged. Accept the reward."

2. Servanthood longevity requires healthy self-care

Many faithful servants get sidelined by a simple problem: too much serving. You heard it here, friends—too much serving. Many new, highly motivated believers doubt that too much service is possible. They quote the writer of Psalm 116:12, "What can I render to the LORD for all his benefits to me?" And they answer, "The more, the better."

"I'd rather burn out than rust out," they say. And all too often that's exactly what they do. They burn out and end up on the sidelines, a serving has-been.

Such a scenario exposes a tragic misunderstanding in the Christian community. *Busyness is next to godliness* sums it up pretty well. Adherents of that way of thinking feel convinced that God favors those who live on the edge of exhaustion and that being at church seven nights a week is a badge of spirituality.

If a friend from their neighborhood or an acquaintance from work calls one of these folks and asks to get together, they can't do it. "Sorry," they say, "I have these eight Christian service things I'm doing, you see, and I just can't waste time on lesser things." Lesser things—like friends, neighbors, spouses, kids, exercise, sleep, recreation, health.

I know. I've been there.

In my youth I had a streak of selfish ambition that had to be broken. I am wired to be very goal-oriented, and I had my goals all mapped out—professional goals, academic goals, financial goals. I knew what I wanted, and I had no intention of letting God or anyone else stand in my way. Something had to break that streak of self-will in me.

God used the self-denial and serve-God-and-other-people verses that Dr. B taught me during the Son City days to begin that process. I memorized those verses. I repeated them every day. It took that kind of determined application of the Word of God to break through the "me-first" mind-set that engulfed me.

But I didn't recognize the difference between self-denial and self-destruction. Self-denial is about denying sin, self-deception, and selfishness. It's about denying whatever God asks us to deny, either through commands in the Bible or through the more personalized direction of the Holy Spirit.

Self-destruction, on the other hand, is about denying authentic feelings, legitimate needs, healthy activities, and life-giving relationships that God never asked us to give up.

Gradually, over the years, I had slid from healthy self-denial into a self-destructive pace of life that pushed me so far into burnout that I feared I would have to leave the ministry.

And I was not the only one who suffered because of the pace of my life. I carry with me the painful reminder that during the highly unbalanced serving era of the '70s, a few young couples in our church ended up divorced because they emulated the unhealthy pace of life that I modeled. I know in my head that God has forgiven me, but I will never get over the sadness that accompanies those memories. I did not realize then that we will all stand as accountable before God for the way we serve at home as we will for how we serve in the church or community, and that caring for those we love is a necessary component of serving longevity.

Remember, the life of servanthood isn't a sprint, but a marathon. In addition to pacing ourselves for the long haul and attending to marriage and family, we need to pay attention to our diet, exercise, and rest. I learned the hard way that if I'm not eating, exercising, and sleeping properly, I will run down physically. And if I'm not enjoying times of recreation and relaxation, I will run down emotionally.

"Serve the LORD with gladness," says the psalmist. "Come into his presence with singing." If you're trying as best you can to do that, but your joy in life is being swallowed by a growing bitterness against the God you claim to love, that may be a tip-off that you're denying more than he is asking you to deny or pacing yourself unrealistically.

Many Christians see only two options: self-centeredness or selflessness. But anyone who is truly selfless all the time will probably end up in an institution. The middle ground of self-care is essential for preserving our giftedness, our sanity, our relationships, and our health so that we can engage in continued service.

There is no one-size-fits-all formula for how to do this, but the Holy Spirit is available to guide us every day as we journal and pray, yielding our lives to God and asking for wisdom and direction.

A friend said, "Radical self-sacrifice requires radical self-care." It's true. If you have been neglecting yourself, thinking you can be a hero and defy the realities of life, you're in dangerous territory. Self-care is not an option. It is the antidote to exhaustion, broken relationships, and burnout, and a necessary component in the life of a joyful, effective, long-term servant of Christ who will one day hear the words, "Well done, my good and faithful servant."

3. Sustained servanthood flows from spiritual fullness

In other words, our serving needs to be properly fueled. We need to pay careful attention to what is motivating us spiritually. Is it guilt? Is it an attempt to earn God's favor? Is it a response to the expectations of others? A need to appear impressive? A need to be needed? If so, serving is ultimately going to become a drudgery, a have-to, a drain.

Sincere, energized servanthood must flow from an ongoing, daily experience of God's presence and love. Spiritual disciplines like solitude, silence, meditation on Scripture, journaling, and prayer keep us grounded, not just in the intellectual truth of God's love, but in the experiential reality of it. Such disciplines open our hearts so that the love of God can speak to us, comfort us, challenge us, and fill us. Then the overflow of that love can spill out into acts of service and love for others. If we are frenetically serving God but never taking the time to commune with him, we may make it through a fifty-yard dash, but we'll never know the joy of finishing the serving marathon to which God calls us.

I don't know how much time I have left on this earth. But I do know what I want to do with that time. I want to serve God with people I love. I want to celebrate the miracle of transformed lives. I want to take good care of my body and my soul. I want to love my family. And every day I want to be filled to overflowing with the love of God. Then, when the time comes for me to cross to the other side, I want to thank God for giving me a life far better than I deserved . . . a life I wouldn't trade for the world.

CHAPTER 11

The Power
of Doing Good

And let us consider how we may spur one another
on toward love and good deeds.

HEBREWS 10:24

But as for you, brethren, do not grow weary of doing good.

2 THESSALONIANS 3:13

In the same way, let your light shine before men, that they
may see your good deeds and praise your Father in heaven.

MATTHEW 5:16

This is a trustworthy statement; and concerning these things
I want you to speak confidently, so that those who have believed
God may be careful to engage in good deeds.

TITUS 3:8

GOOD DEEDS. SPUR ONE ANOTHER ON TOWARD GOOD DEEDS. Do not grow weary of doing good deeds. Let your light shine by doing good deeds. Offer good deeds to all people. Let all those who believe in God engage in good deeds.

Good deeds.

In the Apostle Paul's first letter to Timothy, he tells rich people not to put their hope in wealth, but "to do good, to be rich in good deeds, and to be generous and willing to share ... so that they may take hold of the life that is truly life" (1 Timothy 6:17–19).

In the Gospel of Luke, Jesus commands us to deal with our enemies by doing good to them (Luke 6:31–35).

Paul says to the Romans, "If your enemy is hungry, feed him; if he is thirsty, give him something to drink ... Do not be overcome by evil, but overcome evil with good" (Romans 12:20–21).

Overcome evil with good.

I do not need to waste words, making a case for the evil in our world. For the brokenness. For the pain. For the wars. For poverty. For hunger. For hatred. For greed. For broken families. For the neglected elderly. For the lack of something as basic as clean water for much of the world's population. For loneliness. For abuse of the environment. For the tragedy of AIDS. For spiritual emptiness.

That case is made daily on the evening news—and daily in the men, women, and children whose paths cross ours, if we have eyes to see it.

This book, ultimately, is about the other side of the story. The power of doing good.

Ponder one simple story of that power at work.

After living in a small town house for five years, Jeff and his wife, Karen, wanted to move so they could start a family. Unfortunately, they couldn't find anything they liked in their price range. The situation got complicated because Jeff was working on a long consulting job that wouldn't pay until completion. To make matters worse, the condo association where they lived added a significant expense to their budget by making them replace their garage doors.

They felt ecstatic when Jeff finally finished the consulting job; now they could replace the garage doors and buy a house. "But," explained Jeff, "we believe the 'first fruits' are the Lord's and he put it on our hearts to also purchase the garage doors for two of our neighbors who were struggling to get by. One had cancer; the other just had difficulty paying the bills each month. When we made the presentation of the garage doors to our neighbors, we also shared the story of the Lord's blessing in our lives."

It was then that the Lord "opened the storehouse" for Jeff and Karen. "We were filled to overflowing by the response of our neighbors and by the spiritual awakening in our own hearts, as well. When you are squarely in God's service, you have a feeling that compares to no other and makes you hungry for more."

Within a week, they found their future home. Karen commented, "God had something for us to do before we could move on." It was a powerful lesson.

"Now we ask freely," she says, "*What do you want us to do?* We know that God has a plan and we are part of it."

A simple thing. No complicated plan. No organizational structure. Just a nudge from the Holy Spirit. An act of generosity. Can you imagine what it felt like to be that neighbor struggling with cancer? Or the one who never had quite enough to cover the bills?

Garage doors.

Good deeds.

Or how about this story?

Bob, in his seventies, volunteers in our children's ministry. One Sunday morning, the parents of a little girl did not show up after the service. As Bob waited, the child asked if he would read to her the story of *Winnie the Pooh*. When he finished reading, she asked him to read it again. It puzzled him when she asked a third time, but he started reading despite his growing concern at the parents' delay. Finally, he caught sight of the mother as she entered the room. She stood quietly behind them until he had finished reading.

After they finished one more round of the Pooh, she apologized for being late and thanked him. Then she added: "I was watching, but I did not want to break it up. You are the only man who has read to her since my husband died two years ago."

One elderly gentleman reading *Winnie the Pooh*. Balm for a little girl's soul.

Good deeds.

Do you think that in a world as needy as ours, one person cannot make a difference? On the contrary, every day we have the opportunity to create a world more in keeping with the values we hold dear.

> Not only does each of your actions have a direct impact on the world, but also every choice you make sends a message to those around you . . . We create momentum for each other . . . Don't ever let anyone convince you that you have no power—together we have the power to change the world. All significant changes in the world start slowly, at a single time and place, with a single action. One man, one woman, one child stands up and commits to creating a better world. Their courage inspires others, who begin to stand up themselves. You can be that person.[6]

You can be that person. Do you believe that?

Scott felt moved by the plight of Somali Bantu refugee families relocating in the Chicago area. After ten years in Kenyan refugee camps, the Muslim refugee families would arrive at Chicago's O'Hare Airport with the clothes on their backs and literally nothing else. Scott and his wife, Laurie, decided to "adopt" a particular family—the Muya family—gathering clothes, shoes, winter coats, linens, kitchen supplies, furniture, everything to get them started in an apartment in a Chicago suburb.

As news about the Muya family began to circulate, other people got involved. One family offered to let the Muyas—all eleven of them!—stay in their home for two weeks until their apartment was ready. Other volunteers signed up "round the clock" to help the Muyas navigate a new world of indoor plumbing and electric lights and washing machines and grocery stores and the English language. Within days of their arrival, more than thirty people had joined "Team Bantu." Now, with the Muya family settled into two adjoining apartments, members of "Team Bantu" visit each weekend for tutoring sessions, trips to the Laundromat, and grocery shopping. Others are helping them find jobs.

Scott and Laurie have now cleared a room in their home so they can more proactively gather and store items for other incoming refugees. Under their leadership, "Team Bantu" continues to grow as others catch their vision of being "Christ-reflecting-come-alongside" friends to African refugees.

One couple took a simple action. They started gathering necessary supplies for a family. They didn't know where it would lead. They knew they didn't have room in their home to house a family. They knew that as full-time, employed people they couldn't take on the responsibility of meeting all the daily needs of an incoming family. So they did what they could do. They gathered supplies. But that action spurred others on to good deeds.

Who knows how many refugee families and how many volunteers will be impacted—transformed—by this simple chain of loving actions?

Good deeds.

"I am an old man now," Kevin wrote to me,

> but I have spent the last forty-five years of my life serving the poor and sharing the love of Jesus with the brokenhearted and hurting people of the world. I have walked the streets of Calcutta, Cairo, Chicago, and many other cities, feeding the poor and bringing hope to those with no hope. I wouldn't change what I have done for a million dollars. Tell the people it is worth every ounce of energy spent, every dollar given, every heartache experienced, to see people transformed by the power of the gospel.

Good deeds come in all shapes and sizes. Sometimes they involve garage doors. Sometimes they gravitate toward Winnie the Pooh. Sometimes they look toward Africa. Sometimes they reach all over the world. But in all cases they require one essential thing: a willing volunteer.

Why don't you be that volunteer?

The title of this book calls for a volunteer revolution. Every revolution demands revolutionaries, high-spirited people who dream of a day when things will be different, better. But revolutionaries do more than dream. They give their best to the cause. They relentlessly serve the collective effort.

Imagine what would happen in our world if hundreds of thousands of people—and eventually millions—decided to devote just a few hours each week to generating a wave of good works that would put faith into action and spread goodwill and alleviate suffering.

Imagine if every church and every charitable organization were suddenly inundated with enthusiastic, skilled, loving volunteers who plan, serve, and pray to see a bit more of heaven happening on planet earth. Just imagine!

All that is needed is a ragtag group of spirited revolutionaries who believe it can happen and are willing to take a first step. Do something, somewhere, now, says my friend Jerry. I think that's the perfect battle cry for the volunteer revolution.

Do Something, Somewhere—Now!

I'm pretty sure there's a good deed out there with your name written all over it.

Notes

1. Steve Sjogren, general editor, *Seeing Beyond Church Walls* (Loveland, Colo.: Group Publishing, 2002), 39.

2. The editors, *Spirituality and Health* (May–June 2003), 29.

3. Alan Luks, *Spirituality and Health* (May–June 2003), 34.

4. Stephen Kiesling, *Spirituality and Health* (May–June 2003), 36.

5. Howard Snyder, *Liberating the Church* (Downers Grove, Ill.: InterVarsity, 1983), 169.

6. Ellis Jones, Ross Haenfler, and Brett Johnson with Brian Klocke, *The Better World Handbook,* (Gabriola Island, British Columbia, Canada: New Society Publishers, 2001), 6.

Willow Creek Association

Vision, Training, Resources for Prevailing Churches

This resource was created to serve you and to help you build a local church that prevails. It is just one of many ministry tools that are part of the Willow Creek Resources® line, published by the Willow Creek Association together with Zondervan.

The Willow Creek Association (WCA) was created in 1992 to serve a rapidly growing number of churches from across the denominational spectrum that are committed to helping unchurched people become fully devoted followers of Christ. Membership in the WCA now numbers over 10,000 Member Churches worldwide from more than ninety denominations.

The Willow Creek Association links like-minded Christian leaders with each other and with strategic vision, training, and resources in order to help them build prevailing churches designed to reach their redemptive potential. Here are some of the ways the WCA does that.

- **Prevailing Church Conference**—an annual two-and-a-half day event, held at Willow Creek Community Church in South Barrington, Illinois, to help pioneering church leaders raise up a volunteer core while discovering new and innovative ways to build prevailing churches that reach unchurched people.

- **Leadership Summit**—a once-a-year, two-and-a-half-day conference to envision and equip Christians with leadership gifts and responsibilities. Presented live at Willow Creek as well as via satellite broadcast to over sixty locations across North America, this event is designed to increase the leadership effectiveness of pastors, ministry staff, volunteer church leaders, and Christians in the marketplace.

- **Ministry-Specific Conferences**—throughout each year the WCA hosts a variety of conferences and training events—both at Willow Creek's main campus and offsite, across the U.S. and around the world—targeting church leaders in ministry-specific areas such as: evangelism, the arts, children, students, small groups, preaching and teaching, spiritual formation, spiritual gifts, raising up resources, etc.

- **Willow Creek Resources®**—to provide churches with trusted and field-tested ministry resources in such areas as leadership, evangelism, spiritual formation, spiritual gifts, small groups, stewardship, student ministry, children's ministry, the use of the arts—drama, media, contemporary music—and more. For additional information about Willow Creek Resources® call the Customer Service Center at 800-570-9812. Outside the U.S. call 847-765-0070.

- *WillowNet*—the WCA's Internet resource service, which provides access to hundreds of transcripts of Willow Creek messages, drama scripts, songs, videos, and multimedia tools. The system allows users to sort through these elements and download them for a fee. Visit us online at www.willowcreek.com.

- *WCA News*—a quarterly publication to inform you of the latest trends, resources, and information on WCA events from around the world.

- *Defining Moments*—a monthly audio journal for church leaders featuring Bill Hybels and other Christian leaders discussing probing issues to help you discover biblical principles and transferable strategies to maximize your church's redemptive potential.

- *The Exchange*—our online classified ads service to assist churches in recruiting key staff for ministry positions.

- **Member Benefits**—includes substantial discounts to WCA training events, a 20 percent discount on all Willow Creek Resources®, access to a Members-Only section on WillowNet, monthly communications, and more. Member Churches also receive special discounts and premier services through WCA's growing number of ministry partners—Select Service Providers.

For specific information about WCA membership, upcoming conferences, and other ministry services contact:

Willow Creek Association
P.O. Box 3188, Barrington, IL 60011-3188
Phone: 847-570-9812
Fax: 847-765-5046
www.willowcreek.com

We want to hear from you. Please send your comments about this book to us in care of zreview@zondervan.com. Thank you.

GRAND RAPIDS, MICHIGAN 49530 USA

WWW.ZONDERVAN.COM